# THE BOOK OF
# WORST MEALS

# THE BOOK OF WORST MEALS

25 Authors Write about Terrible
Culinary Experiences

Edited by Walter Cummins
and Thomas E. Kennedy

**SERVING HOUSE BOOKS**

The Book of Worst Meals:
25 Authors Write about Terrible Culinary Experiences

ISBN: 978-0-9826921-2-7

Serving House Books logo by Barry Lereng Wilmont

Published by Serving House Books

www.servinghousebooks.com

First Edition 2010

*The food here is terrible, and the portions are too small.*
                                                    —*Woody Allen*

# Contents

9    Introduction

13    Martin Donoff, *A Turbid Stew of Quivering Flotsam*

23    Ellen Visson, *Une Américaine en Brochette: Dining in Switzerland during the Cold War*

33    Terrence Kerrigan, *Eating Italian in Paris with Stanley Elkin and* Candy

43    Gladys Swan, *The Savor of Experience*

49    Duff Brenna, *Sneeze Dressing & Caribou Gravy*

61    Dennys Khomate, *Danish Christmas Lunch*

69    Thomas McCarthy, *Breakfast in Brighton*

75    Mimi Schwartz, *There but for the Grace: First Thanksgiving*

81    Steve Davenport, *Bang, Boot, Man, Woman*

87    Renée Ashley, *Her Very Worst Meal and How It Was Much Like the Three Fat Men—One of Whom Was Wearing a Beret— She Saw Today*

93    Susan Tekulve, *Hell Broth & Poisoned Entrails: An Affair with Scottish Cookery*

101    Wallis Wilde-Menozzi, *A Flood of Doom*

105    Victor Rangel-Ribeiro, *Honeymoon Dinner on Mahabaleshwar Mountain*

113    Peter Selgin, *The Duchess Flounder*

119    R.A. Rycraft, *Firsts & Seconds*

125    Rick Mulkey, *The Best They Had To Offer*

131    Alexandra Marshall, "*Sukiyaki Song*"

137    Catherine Doty, *Gnaw Thanks*

141    Lisa del Rosso, *Kosher Blues*

147    Walter Cummins, *Vile Memories*

149      Sudeep Sen, *Carving Salmon*

151      Kenneth Smoady, *The Food Wars of My Childhood*

155      Sean Finucane Toner, *The Quarter Million Dollar Chicken Filet*

161      Thomas E. Kennedy, *Portuguese Garden Buffet*

167      Michael Lee, *Stepping over the Velvet Rope*

173      About the Editors

173      Contributors

# Introduction

Authors relish the opportunity to write about food, verbally luxuriating over the details of a meal as if devouring their imagined menus through the fingertips that hold a pen or tap a keyboard. They serve their readers festive tables, fulfilled appetites, ecstatic diners, and even spiritual transformations.

Charles Dickens offers pages of Victorian abundance and overflowing platters. One of his early pieces, "A Christmas Dinner" of 1835, typifies the meals to come in his fiction:

> As to the dinner, it's perfectly delightful - nothing goes wrong, and everybody is in the very best of spirits, and disposed to please and be pleased. Grandpapa relates a circumstantial account of the purchase of the turkey, with a slight digression relative to the purchase of previous turkeys, on former Christmas-days, which grandmamma corroborates in the minutest particular. Uncle George tells stories, and carves poultry, and takes wine, and jokes with the children at the side-table, and winks at the cousins that are making love, or being made love to, and exhilarates everybody with his good humour and hospitality; and when, at last, a stout servant staggers in with a gigantic pudding, with a sprig of holly in the top, there is such a laughing, and shouting, and clapping of little chubby hands, and kicking up of fat dumpy legs, as can only be equalled by the applause with which the astonishing feat of pouring lighted brandy into mince-pies, is received by the younger visitors.

But plump fowl and huge desserts aren't always necessary. Marcel Proust, well-known for the powers of a madeleine, again reveals the transformative wonders of even a bite and a sip in this passage from Swan's Way:

And soon, mechanically, dispirited after a dreary day with the prospect of a depressing morrow, I raised to my lips a spoonful of the tea in which I had soaked a morsel of the cake. No sooner had the warm liquid mixed with the crumbs touched my palate than a shudder ran through me and I stopped, intent upon the extraordinary thing that was happening to me. An exquisite pleasure had invaded my senses, something isolated, detached, with no suggestion of its origin. And at once the vicissitudes of life had become indifferent to me, its disasters innocuous, its brevity illusory - this new sensation having had on me the effect which love has of filling me with a precious essence; or rather this essence was not in me, it was me. I had ceased now to feel mediocre, contingent, mortal. Whence could it have come to me, this all-powerful joy?

In Denmark, it is said that if you see a group of people standing close together and speaking intensely, if you move close, you are as likely as not to hear one of them saying, "And then we had... And then we had...," describing a wonderful meal, course by course, in glowing gustatory recollection.

Food such as this is not representative of our day-to-day fare. The forgettable stuff we usually eat certainly doesn't inspire such passages, at most dismissed with "Her breakfast was a prune Danish and a cup of coffee" or "He wolfed down a burger and fries."

But what of meals that are a culinary nightmare, experiences of unforgettable awfulness? Not merely bad food but bad food eaten with bad company in bad circumstances? Don't they deserve descriptions? Paragraphs that may serve as therapy or retribution or purgation?

In this collection, a group of writers have welcomed the opportunity to tell the world of not just any bad meal but of the very worst experienced in all their lives, seared into their most negative and painful memories. I suppose we could say read it and retch. But we expect most who pick up this book to be relieved that it wasn't them and actually find amusement in the sufferings of others. And why not? To paraphrase Mel Brooks, tragedy is when you swallow swill, comedy is when someone else does.

May we all dine on plump plum puddings and digest all-powerful joy.

—Walter Cummins
—Thomas E. Kennedy

# A Turbid Stew of Quivering Flotsam

*Martin Donoff*

I am sitting at a kitchen table, a mid-century dinette set, looking down at a pile of gelatinous pasta topped with fried balls of Spam and ketchup. The Beatles are still together, students are not rioting in Paris and no one has yet set foot on the moon. To my left is a dour, middle-aged man who is probably guessing what his daughter and I do when he's not around. To my right is a stolid, middle-aged woman who probably knows, but doesn't want to think about, what her daughter and I do. And the object of all my lust sits across from me, happily twirling ketchup-laden spaghetti onto her fork, spearing a nugget of Spam ball and placing it in her mouth. I follow her example and moments later I wonder just how I got here.

"Come have dinner with my family," she said, adjusting her swimsuit and bringing into view the horizontal tan line just below her sacral dimples. I'm transfixed. Come to dinner? Kiss a cobra? Take up with the flagellants? Yep. Sure. You bet. "You'll love my mother's spaghetti," she adds.

And now, with a mouthful of the beloved pasta, I finally understand how awful got such a bad reputation.

"Waddya think?" my girlfriend asks.

I swallow and turn toward the Mother. "This is delicious," I lie. "Can you give me the recipe for my mother?"

"Oh, it's just Spam and some ketchup," she says. "And, you have to make sure to cook the noodles until they're really done —almost smooth."

I pause to consider the strategy for the next mouthful.

"Aren't you going to tell him the secret ingredient?" Father asks.

"He'll just have to come back for that," Mother says and winks at me.

I take the next mouthful, suppress the rising gorge, and wonder what is happening. I'm eating execrable food; I've turned into a smarmy, obsequious liar; I've learned that the woman I desire above all things has no taste and, at 17, I've just discovered the character flaw that will probably destroy the rest of my life. I'll eat shit to get laid.

It's a flaw as tragic as Oedipus. And if he cut out his eyes, what am I going to have to cut out or off? Why have I been brought here to end my days so young? What have I done to these people to make them do this to me?

And then Mother picks up a pitcher and pours milk into my empty glass. I don't drink milk, but she doesn't know that. The spaghetti is inedible, but she doesn't know that either. It's an innocent mistake and, like all food we offer to guests, a gesture of kindness and I forgive her. I forgive Father, too, for having the grace to sit at the same table with me even though he probably thinks that my left hand isn't really politely in my lap but slipping up his daughter's thigh. And I forgive my girlfriend for her tanned neck and her sacral dimples and the extraordinary shade of grey-green eyes that I stare into for the rest of dinner.

§

We're sitting on wooden café chairs and there's a red-checkered tablecloth. It's a cliché and she's made her feelings known about that. The waiter, a student at the Academy of Vocal Arts, has just finished singing *O Soave Fanciulla* to a recorded background and tells us he'll be right back with our dinner. This, too, annoys my companion. She wants to know if he is going to sing all night? "Every time I want something, is he going to stop and break into song?" In fact there's not much she likes about anything on this first date. The place is too warm, the tables too close, the menu too rustic. She seems to have complaints with other parts of her life as well. With no prior training she auditioned for The Actor's Studio, was accepted and now complains about how hard it is.

"It's wonderful training," I say. "You know all the great actors who got their start there."

"It's all reputation," she responds. "I don't think they get what I'm doing. They never praise anything. They just ask about my motivations and choices, motivations and choices. Shit, everything's a choice and every action has a motivation. Do you really like this place?"

"Yes. It's corny, but it's fun. And the food is pretty good. Try to get into the spirit."

"The spirit of the guy spilling sauce on a napkin tucked under his chin?" She gestures toward the older man at the next table. His hands shake as he eats. "You're not going to do that, are you? Christ, that would embarrass the hell out of me."

Our waiter returns with her salad and my Spaghetti Caruso. My date grimaces. "What's on your pasta?"

"Chicken livers and wild mushrooms."

"You're going to eat that?"

Before I can respond a waiter at the front of the room cues up a record and launches into the opening siciliana from *Cavalleria Rusticana*. Nearly everyone smiles, drinks, eats, listens and applauds when he's done. My date taps her fork on the table. "Again, the singing. What if you don't understand Italian?"

I offer a rough translation of some of the lyrics; Lola's illicit lover leaving in the morning, singing about seeing her red and pink through her nightgown, claiming he won't enter Paradise if she's not there. It's erotic and a bit romantic, too.

"Do you think that stuff turns a woman on? It's way over the top. Let's have some champagne."

"I don't think they have any. "

"Yeah, they do. I saw it on the wine list."

I don't want to order champagne for her. I want to concentrate on my food and forget she's here. But I can't. I'm going to make what I can of the evening. So I order a bottle of champagne and promise myself I'll forget this night and won't be the kind of jerk who needs revenge and tells everyone about her.

Her name is Karen and she lives in Philadelphia.

Near the art museum.

In a brownstone.

There's a stained glass bird above the painted wood door.

It's blue.

§

There are seven of us at a round table in the Executive Dining Room because the Vice President of Promotion insists it's better than any restaurant in town and private so we can talk. It's all men and I'll be reporting to two of them if I get and take the job. Although it's only a three-month write and shoot, I really want to keep working during this TV hiatus and so I'm being careful in this company. I'd hoped everyone would settle for a simple lunch or a sandwich, but it's appetizers and entrees all around. I guess it's a Midwestern thing, a full dinner at lunchtime. I follow suit and try to play it safe with the petit crabcakes on a bed of mache greens and, from the daily specials list, Patrick's Irish Stew. I assume Patrick is the chef and that he's Irish. I hope he's not the Asian busboy.

Ten minutes of conversation go by without any obvious traps. It doesn't feel like an interrogation and my worries about seeming too Eastern (or, worse still, too West Coast-Entertainment Business) are probably unfounded. And then I smell something. I'm not sure at first, but I'm getting a peculiar sense of under-the-boardwalk at low tide. And there's something else— sharp and musky. Across the room our waiter, tray in hand, has just come from the kitchen and he's headed our way. And now he's behind me. And now he reaches over my shoulder and puts the crabcakes down in front of me. And now I can identify the aroma—it's the dumpster near the parking lot behind Mel's Crab Shack, Anywhere-by-the-Sea, New Jersey. The sharp and musky smell is the dusting of Old Bay seasoning on these very old crab cakes.

I ask the waiter for horseradish and, after he serves the rest of the table, he goes off to get it. "Please enjoy," the VP says and gestures for all of us to begin. Everyone picks up their forks. Then they notice that my hands are in my lap.

"Please start," I say. "I really love horseradish with my crabcakes. It's become a fetish." And I tell them the story of my immigrant grandfather making his own horseradish in the basement. At family dinners he'd bring it upstairs in a prized, cut-glass bowl. As soon as it entered the room our sinuses would clear. We'd put a polite dab on our plates and avoid letting any food touch it. My grandfather would take a forkful and exclaim, "It's weak, too weak."

Everyone is smiling and I think I'm off the hook about the horseradish. "Funny how all those immigrant food stories are about smell," the IBM suit to my left says. "Those tenements must have really stunk to high heaven."

I'm not sure how to respond but the VP saves me. "I don't suppose your grandfather left his horseradish grinder to you?" he asks.

"No, I think it had to be buried with him." I secretly hope that my grandfather is back from the dead and grinding incredibly hot horseradish in the Executive Dining room kitchen.

The waiter returns with a ramekin of the jarred, purplish concoction that passes for horseradish. I spoon two tablespoons onto my plate and try to get a large portion of horseradish with every mouthful. It barely begins to cover the taste and oilcloth texture of the very old crab.

The conversation grows bland—generic thoughts and comments about the Super Bowl and kids in school. They ask me softball questions about the TV shows I've worked on. They're not looking for revelations or even information, just trying to see if I can fit in. If I am simpatico with their world view.

I eat only as much crabcake as the horseradish will cover and leave a small portion on the plate. No one seems to notice. The busboy clears the plates just as the waiter shows up with the entrees. I haven't smelled anything in advance this time, so I'm hopeful. He reaches over my shoulder and puts a green crockery bowl with a white lid in front of me, places a new fork and soupspoon to the right and lifts the lid. There are string beans standing straight upright in the bowl, held in that position by pearlescent globules of congealing fat. They stand sentry around large chunks of lamb, or perhaps mutton, most of which are still enrobed in silver-white fell. A few desultory, grayish potatoes bob up and down nearby while three chunks of carrot, cooked to gray and looking for all the world like hooded druids, circle head-down in the murky, thick brown liquid.

"Looks just like the Irish stew my aunt Natalia used to make," the IBM suit says.

"Your aunt Natalia was Irish?" the VP asks.

"No, Romanian."

Everybody laughs. I do too, even though the joke seems to be rehearsed.

"And what does a Romanian put into Irish stew?" someone asks.

"Stolen horsemeat."

Now they're all laughing louder. It's obviously a routine and I start to wonder. The guy's name is Cook. Was it originally Cocescu, from a dark mustachioed family known for curing pastrami in their apartment until the floors above and below complained about the pervasive smell of garlic and brine? No, his forbears were all towheaded; grew up in cabins across the prairie where one bad, wet winter when ergot got into the grain stores and mold ruined everything in the root cellar, they brought in Queenie, the plow horse, patted her nose goodbye, slit her throat, pulled out her innards, and skinned and butchered her. What with the blood and the offal slick on the floors it must have started to smell a bit like a tenement. I catch myself here in mid-reverie. Where am I going with this? More to the point, where did the Aunt Natalia joke come from? Maybe this is the real test of simpatico. I'm beginning to wonder if I fit in or want any part of this job.

I decide to divert my concerns with a story about my other grandfather making cherry wishniak and how I tried to get the recipe. He'd macerate cherries in sugar water until they fermented. How many cherries? How much sugar water? "Whatever looks right, he'd say. Then he'd add a bottle of vodka and let it sit until everything was deep red. Finally, he'd top off the jug with whiskey. I'd ask him how big a jug and he'd say, "A jug. You know. A jug—everyone has a jug." I often worried that he meant one of those glass jugs that bleach used to come in. But I guess that when the decoction was finished, the drink was so overpowering that no one ever noticed a chlorine taste.

The VP smirks at my story. "I didn't know your people drank that much. I always admired them for their temperance."

I want to tell him that my people capture and sell gentile children to the matzo factory for whiskey money. Then, all liquored up, they go out looking for young, blonde virgins to defile. They rampage through the amber waves spreading their seed across the prairies, dotting the northern great plains with their outposts— bagels in Bemidji, knishes in Kenosha, smoked salmon in Sioux Ste. Marie. Then down the Big Muddy in kayaks and canoes. Belly full of moonshine, one foot up on the prow, Captain Slipknot Cohen calls out to the mountain men of the Ozarks, "We're coming. Take heart. You won't have to marry your feeble blonde sisters anymore. We're full of potlikker and we'll sodomize them for you. We'll show you pure-blooded Scotch-Irish-German-French-Potawatomies just what mongrelizing is all about. "

What am I doing? Why am I slipping into some dark, fervid corner of my imagination and sending a rabble of Ashkenazi Jews marauding down the Mississippi? It shouldn't take this much anger to make me realize that I don't want this job. I'll finish lunch, the interviews and get the hell out. I'm not gong to respond to his comment. I'm going to take a mouthful of Patrick's Irish stew. I maneuver past the upright beans and spoon up some lamb, potato and liquid and try to parse the tastes. Game, slick grease, wet fur, the forest after a flood and something else, faint but there. I think it's putrefaction. It's a strange, thick, musty sweetness that clings to my palate. I think I can smell it as well as it drifts up to my back olfactory sensors. I wonder if this is what people who are starving and forced to eat rancid meat taste. I wonder if this is what the poor in Victorian England tasted every day.

"You're originally from Philadelphia?" the guy to the left of the VP asks.

I look up and nod but really pay no attention. In the bowl, the liquid is still rippling from the incursion of my spoon and the lamb pieces seem to quiver. The words "turbid stew of quivering flotsam," come to mind in a British accent. Isn't that what Arthur Clennam was served on the night he was accidentally locked in the Marshalsea. Is my lunch from Dickens?

"Have you always lived on the East coast?" he presses on and I think the question is pointed. Is he going to ask if I'm a Democrat? A liberal? The anti-Christ? I think I see an unpleasant grin forming and a small line of spittle at the corners of his mouth.

Am I hallucinating? Can rancid stew cause instant hallucinations? Did I read something about that in one of Castaneda's books? I can't remember. I didn't pay much attention—only read them because a college girlfriend said I was too straight and she wouldn't sleep with me anymore unless I read Castaneda and took mushrooms with her. I read the books, wouldn't take the mushrooms and never saw her naked again.

"Are you allright?" the VP asks, showing some concern that I've stopped answering questions.

I'm not. I'm in the wrong country at a table full of strangers. It's a very bad meal and there's no one I can forgive for an innocent mistake and no one has grey-green eyes that remind me of my high school sweetheart and I'm thinking about rampaging drunken Jews and Charles Dickens and Carlos Castaneda and Little Dorrit and the shaman Don Juan and there's a question that everyone is waiting for me to answer and I have a mouthful of something that no one should ever eat and soon, very soon, I'm going to have to swallow.

# Une Américaine en Brochette: Dining in Switzerland during the Cold War

*Ellen Visson*

It was a dim autumn Tuesday in Geneva, 1983. My fiancé Philip and I had arrived the previous August for two weeks to settle a fatuous lawsuit mounted by two warring galleries around his paintings. We were still there. Our money was running out. And, although we were legally tourists, the head of the Police of Foreigners had ordered us over the telephone in his best Cold-War style to leave the country. Before our arrival, there had been much chicanery around these paintings involving an art agent with double nationality (American and Panamanian); a high-powered Swiss realtor; and a variety of Swiss lawyers, art dealers and museum directors who knew all too well how to sail the surface waters of neutrality while trawling the deep for fatter fare. Hundreds of works had disappeared. Some had been sold and the proceeds, divided into oblivion. It was a scenario scrabbled together by John Le Carré and the Marx Brothers. But that is another story.

The rain dripped from the dying leaves. We were on our way to a luncheon whose curious invitation had arrived by telephone from (we suspected) a spurious Spanish Countess whom we had met at the American Embassy a week before. The Ambassadress—a gracious woman who had once taught Philip, as a child, ballroom dancing— had invited us to a luncheon in Bern at which upon arrival we found the Spanish Countess. Thus our summons a week later in Geneva.

This world was new to me. Philip had been raised in it. His father had been a political analyst with *The Washington Post* and a roving editor of *The Reader's Digest*, a White Russian and one of the original OSS men for the Soviet and Balkans desks. Everyone assumed Philip had gone into the same ambiguous political backwaters; but that was not the case: as a painter and artist, he talked incessantly and could not keep secrets, nor did he want to. This was his natural defense against recruitment of any kind.

I can't recall why we accepted the invitation. I believe the Spanish Countess had once harbored the American / Panamanian art agent in her house, and we hoped to find out what had become of some missing paintings much coveted by certain dealers— artworks that we might then have sold to survive. But in any case, we found ourselves at a round table in the dining room of the Hotel Beau-Rivage in Geneva, and seated—not by the Countess, whom we assumed was the hostess—but instead by a large, white-haired American whose jolly red cheeks and Southern accent belied the ice in his eyes. He seated me on his right. On my other side poised a short man with intense eyes and hollow cheeks who resembled a Russian icon and later confessed to being a defrocked priest. Philip was placed across from me and next to the Countess. On his right was a tidy Swiss woman of the governess variety who hardly spoke but who, with seeming distraction, was intensely present.

The waiter handed out menus. This was to be a three-course French meal with two wines. Everyone decided on the fare of the day. I was a vegetarian, and my request for a substitute received the usual terse suggestion of "*poisson.*" I did not eat fish. "*Omelette*" was the waiter's next suggestion. I didn't eat eggs, either; and we continued down the evolutionary ladder to the inevitable "*assiette de légumes,*" the phrase dry on his tongue. The Swiss governess sighted me over her glasses with a querulous look.

"My dear," she said in her precise English, "you will stunt your growth."

"*Tant mieux*," I said. I was nearly six feet tall and besides, *tant mieux* was one of the few French idioms I had picked up.

The Southerner regarded me with a slanted smile. "Kill or be killed," he said. The invasion of Grenada had just started. "Are you someone we have to report?" he added, his face granite, as if he himself had given the order and was responsible for the latest unrest. I was still reeling from the edict from the Swiss Police of Foreigners, and now it seemed the American services were going to join the powerful officials whom I'd offended. "You surely do *look* guilty," he said. "Are you one of those ex-student *Communist* vegetarians?" And he burst into solitary laughter.

"On the contrary," said the defrocked priest in a heavy Polish accent. He shot me a look of complicity. "Vegetarianism has a long history in the Church. The Trappist, Benedictine and Franciscan traditions are to abstain from meat. *The cow and the bear shall graze, and the lion shall eat straw like the ox.* Even the Hebrew Daniel has given us the example. Some say that the original apple of Adam was the heart of a butchered animal."

The governess shuddered.

"The Church has its share of Communists, too," murmured the Southerner.

Attention turned to Philip, whose mother tongue was French. He had grown up shuttling between Europe and Washington, D.C.—legally a territory where the inhabitants could not yet vote in Presidential elections. Whereas my girlhood had been apolitical, with the usual bicycles merging into a 1959 Chevy Impala and adolescent tantrums, his *jeunesse* had been immersed in the diplomatic and social worlds of both continents. His first exhibition of paintings was at sixteen, in Paris. He had always been an artist.

"We're here to settle a lawsuit and locate some missing paintings," he explained, as ever his heart and our lives stretched along the length of his sleeve. "I hear," he said to the Countess, "that Graham stayed in your house." Graham Tarkington Howard was the American / Panamanian agent who had since vanished.

"Graham?" said the Countess, pausing with her napkin like a barrier before her. She was in her delinquent seventies, and had arrived at the Embassy luncheon in Bern unzipped. When the Ambassador—an old friend—had shyly remarked this, she had asked him to zip her up.

"My agent," continued Philip. "I mentioned him at the Embassy." And to the table in general: "Graham had been on the front page of *The Washington Post* for the creation of some fraudulent check-cashing scheme where millions disappeared. I met him in Washington, he was once the husband of a friend of mine. She introduced us. She said that Graham had been hiding out in Andorra. But I heard," he repeated to the Countess, "that he had stayed in your house for several months."

"I know nothing of your Graham."

"But I heard it from—" and Philip mentioned a publisher's wicked daughter, the most accomplished gossip in Lausanne.

By now the first course had arrived—a *duo de saumon mi-cuit et fumé couché sur une salade frisée à l'huile de noix*, the pinkish-orange flesh of the fish glimmering like a sunset far in the distance. The tablecloth before me shone with void. I did however share the wine. Glasses were raised and health toasted. Philip abstained: as a reformed alcoholic, he had ordered Coca-Cola—very American but still suspect. The two of us were marked.

Forks scraped across plates. Philip continued a monologue again describing how Graham and he had met, and how Graham had since popped up in *The Washington Post* again, this time on a back page as a painter in an international art fair. The title of the article had been "His Best Scam Ever". If information had been the goal of this luncheon, everyone was *bien servi*.

"And did you also know this fascinating Graham?" the defrocked priest asked me.

"Oh yes. I met him in Washington, in 1976. Before he came

here to Switzerland."

"And what does he look like?" The Countess lifted a brow over her aimed eye. The priest cleared his throat. "Perhaps I met him unknowingly," he added.

"Yes, perhaps we all met him unknowingly," the Southerner chuckled. He glanced at the Countess, the corners of his eyes mounted in play.

"Well," I answered. I was trying to buy my way in by being helpful. "He is tall and blond with blue eyes. Innocuous. Handsome in a bland way. Could fit in anywhere."

"That tells me everything and nothing," said the Southerner, looking at me in a new way.

"On the contrary," said the ex-Jesuit. "He sounds like a perfect example of a countryman of yours. And how many typical young Americans do we have here? Not that many, if you examine our streets. Just a few Germans, that's all."

"So your Graham is innocuous," repeated the Southerner, ignoring the remark. "Innocuous people are my specialty." And he smiled kindly at me.

"What about the Swiss Germans," the governess piped in. "They are often tall and blond."

"Ah, but your compatriots are much more intense," replied the ex-priest. "They could be mistaken for Scandinavians escaping from a Bergman film."

Everyone laughed, and chatter became general. I heard something about the new highway and its destruction of the landscape; a referendum by the Swiss population around the quota for real estate sales to foreigners; the sorry state of America after Vietnam; a running dialogue insisting that the wicked daughter of the publisher was trying to sell some fake Dufys; and a statement about a floundering lawyer who had been caught with his eleventh finger in one too many pies—a scandal involving millions but which the Swiss press would ignore because it was a civil and not penal court case.

The main course arrived: *carré de veau rôti aux herbes sur le chariot et son jus, spätzli au beurre, et épinards Montfermeil.* One waiter carved while another heaped up the bleeding slices onto the warm plates. A third perfunctorily served me one half of an endive sliced and fanned out, its leaves dried like tissue onto the plate by the heating lamp in the kitchen. Three cherry tomatoes puckered beside it, and a spear of broccoli completed their pyramid. It felt as if I were being punished. The Countess was having a cozy chat with Philip in French. I could not understand much, but it seemed to be about the American Ambassador.

"He was what? *Comment?*" cried the governess, who had overheard.

"He had been an actor," said Philip in English for my sake, although I knew the story. "He is completely bilingual, having been raised in Europe. He even starred in a film with Marlene Dietrich. *The Scarlet Empress.*"

"An actor appointed by an actor," sneered the governess, a cheek stuffed with roasted veal.

"But he is a wonderful man," protested the Countess. "I knew him when he was acting, you know. I used to be in the theatre myself."

"And that is how you met your husband, the Count," added the Southerner. No one spoke for a moment. A knife screeched across a plate. "What we need to remake America," the Southerner finally remarked, "is a really good war."

A cherry tomato exploded in my mouth. The ex-priest and Countess laughed but no one else did.

"Something to bring us all together after Vietnam," he continued.

"Grenada?" asked the ex-priest, his brows raised but his dark eyes twinkling beneath them.

"No no, not one of these fire-cracker fights—pop, and it's over.

No no. Something fierce to clean out the mess."

Philip and I looked at each other across the table.

"Surely," said the governess, her Swiss neutrality riled, "you can't mean another World War."

The Southerner looked at Philip then at me. "Something like that," he answered. "When I saw combat not a man, woman nor suckling chil' was left in any town we crossed." Silence descended while his white hair glistened under the lights. "There's real manhood for you. None of this Graham salesman stuff or artistic business."

The waiter fussed, pouring more wine around the quiet table. Two men speaking loud Arabic could be heard. I concentrated on the stem of my endive, toughened into cork.

The Countess grinned. "You will have your fun," she said. Everyone but the Southerner agreed with nervous laughter, and stilted conversation wandered across the table again until dessert arrived. Gratefully I concentrated on my *crème brûlée*. The Countess tried regaling us by an account of a tryst with Picasso in Vallauris during his poorer years.

"And did you acquire any works," asked the de-frocked priest.

"Yes. Some pottery. Alas, sold long ago."

We all paused in sympathy to the shared anonymity of money troubles.

Coffee was served. Everyone but the Southerner and de-frocked priest seemed in the trenches, and we held onto our cups as to rifles.

The Countess rallied. "And what," she asked Philip, "do you paint?"

His eyes opened in Slavic innocence. "But surely you saw some work when Graham was in your house. I thought you still had about fifty paintings stored there. At least, that's what I heard." And he named again the naughty daughter of the publisher.

"I've already told you, I don't know any Graham." She churned into a shade of pink. "You artists are all *fantaisistes*. Fabricators."

29

"But—"

"Between imagination and reality there is a huge gap."

"And where does reality start," deflected the ex-priest. "Where do we begin to believe you," he said to Philip, "about your Graham—and you—" to the Countess, "about your Picasso? When can we even trust our own memories?"

"Just so," said the Countess, eyeing Philip.

"And you," he said to the Southerner, "about your war?"

"Oh you can believe me about my war."

The governess tut-tutted.

"I believe you," I said.

"Reality," said the Southerner, "is not the bullshit you read in the papers. Reality is all about what seems most untrue."

"How right you are," cried the de-frocked priest, his iconesque quality shining through. "Reality is not what we see or feel or touch. *God is a Spirit*."

"Bollocks," said the Countess, who must have learned her English in Britain. "So when," she turned to me, "are you going back to America?"

I looked at Philip. "I am applying for a living permit," he said.

The Countess smiled. "Surely you can't both be thinking of staying here. You know how hard it is to get landed, even for a single person. Do you have job offers?" Her eyes batted in mock concern. "Then how will the two of you survive on paintings? Your girlfriend must have a fortune." She looked at me with new interest.

I had no fortune, and the impossibility of our future loomed once more before me. "Reality is about what seems most untrue," I found myself saying.

The Southerner turned red with hilarity.

"Why doesn't everyone come to my house for a liqueur?" interjected the Countess. And she laid a practiced hand upon my fiancé's.

Everyone agreed except Philip, who spoke of a previous

engagement. He was a bad liar and his untruth seemed to disband the party. For whose benefit or for what purpose it had been formed, we were never to know.

# Eating Italian in Paris with Stanley Elkin and *Candy*

*Terrence Kerrigan*

> *"Good grief —it's daddy!"*
> —*Maxwell Kenton,* Candy

Paris! A bandoneon echoing through the metro station St. Paul playing—could it be? Yes!—"Under Paris Skies," which you first heard when you were, like, six years old on the radio in Queens and were transported into the dreamy nostalgic womb of sound (you have since decided this memory must be at least partially Oedipal since your mother's maiden name was Paris). *Sous le Ciel de Paris...* You emerge on Rue de Rivoli. Quatrième Arrondisement. It is early February. Large heavy snowflakes slant, softly falling, and you step carefully over the slick cobblestones toward the hotel on rue de Jarente.

In the lobby as you wait to check in, you look through the many shelves of books there, gathered apparently for the pleasure of the guests. Mostly in English and among the usual suspects -- the Grisham's and King's and Clancy's and Steele's—you spy a Kafka, a McEwan, a Cormac McCarthy, even Maxwell Kenton's *Candy* (first published and banned in Paris!), even by god a Stanley Elkin! Your room is on the fourth floor, and it is perfectly *Parisienne*: on the salmon-colored wall, a picture frame of heavy duct tape patterned to resemble carved wood framing a large blank rectangle of salmon-colored wall; the small flat-screen TV stands on a badly hand-painted blue wooden table with a drawer, its pull knob of plastic imitation crystal. The TV, of course, does not work. In the bathroom two plastic toothbrush glasses, one translucent blue, one translucent pink. A rickety chair and desk in an alcove beneath the pictureless faux picture-frame. The chair, as you tentatively lower your butt to it, threateningly sighs and trembles; you rise again like a shot and notice above the bed pictures of yachts in full sail against a hard summer wind, two of a pale blue series. In the corner, of course, an enormous, lopsided armoire of solid wood looks dour as its age, feeling the pains of its many years in this room behind the spotted lacy curtains that protect one from the intruding eyes of whoever lives on the other side of the narrow rue de Jarente. Yes, the room is perfect. You'll take it. In fact, you already took it and ordered breakfast in the "dining room" at eight which you know will be served by a smiling woman of indeterminate age who has no English and delivers, on a plain white paper setting, a small metal pot of coffee and smaller, spoutless impossible-to-pour pot of *lait chaud*, a six-inch long segment of yesterday's baguette, a tiny jar of marmalade, a glass of ersatz juice. *Parfait, madame, merci beaucoup, vous etes très gentile!*

*Ah, monsieur,* she says and something else you do not understand. Perhaps, You are teasing me, monsieur. Or, *It is a hungry dance we do along the blade of monsieur's sword.*

Your French is nearly as little as her English, and the two of you will have a blessed conversation over the next three days, smiling at one another past the wordless barrier. *Madame, may I tickle you a leetle bit.* But apparently she thinks you are just asking for a croissant and replies, *"Pas croissant, monsieur—plus de pain?"*

You had forgotten. That of all the cities upon this earth Paris is the capital of everything. Even if you barely scratch the surface. Paris is the city of light, the city of romance, the city of the bandoneon, the city of haughty unapproachable beautiful women and the city

34

of the unexpected smile, the city of bookshops for no one in the world loves reading more than Parisians, not even Dubliners, and it is the city in which everything—every single thing—that you eat is delicious, be it a simple green salad, *crudités*, be it raw *huitres* on the half shell with a flute of champagne, be it any of the nation's four hundred cheeses, be it.... Well, no, don't think of Italian just now, no don't think of that. Your pleura still ache. Think rather of Stanley Elkin—of how Helen Vendler describes in her introduction to his *Pieces of Soap* the way he translates pity and fear into mockery and terror. Think how Stanley got you through with self-mockery the night of terror that would confront you the day after.

Think rather of how you walked into the hotel lobby with snow on the shoulders of your leather coat and the *Parisienne* behind the desk looked up smiling vaguely to say, "Ah! It is snewing!" And you saw in her Gallic grey eyes that the two of you shared that childish delight and insuperable belief that snow will transform the world and make it pure.

Think rather of walking along the Seine toward *Ile de la Cité*, sneaking up on the rear flanks of *Notre Dame*, its jutting gargoyles like—admit it!—stiff pricks. Think of how the snow looked slanting into the brown-green Seine, making you think of a francophone version of "The Dead"—*Snow was general all over France...* Think of your delight to discover on rue Saint Paul a bookshop you did not know existed, The Red Wheelbarrow Bookstore which could only, of course, be Anglophone (*It is a serious dance we do along the blade of monsieur's sword!*) so you went in, not daring to quote to the beautiful shop attendant your parody of William Carlos Williams: *Those plums? That you were saving in the fridge? Screw you, I ate 'em!* Instead you make *le chit-chat* and seeing she is receptive, that she smiles at you to warm your heart, perhaps thinking you a quaint old cat in your beret and long grey scarf, and you ask where she is from, and she says New York, the west side. And you say, Ah, the real New York—I was but a resident of Queens. And she hastens with her big smile and big auburn hair to assure you that she was born in Forest Hills, and you are off remembering that you once had a girlfriend in Forest Hills. With auburn hair much like your own, *chère Madame*. You were 16, she 14. It was 1960. You took her to the—*comment-dit-on*—*les movies*, and you sat with her in the balcony and the film was wonderful; fifteen minutes into it, you leaned over to kiss her and she let you, and you didn't stop kissing her or she you for three weeks. She was a girl much like you, *chère madame*, almost as beautiful.

Think rather of how four of you gathered on the Contrescarpe at the café which used to be called Café La Chope where Ernest Hemingway, who lived around the corner on the rue Descartes, because he only had enough money either to heat his room or spend the day in the café, chose the latter, writing about Jake Barnes and drinking rum. And wouldn't it be pretty to think of how you and Bob and Lisa and Jessie and Dave gathered there and talked the afternoon away as the snow slanted across the square, remembering another afternoon nine years before when you thought you were old but were actually young and gathered with Walt and Alison and three Davids and a Janet and others and drank away a summer afternoon...

Think of this and so much more. Think of the meal at Le Petit Zinc on rue Saint-Benoît—the oysters, the cheeses, the tart! The champagne flutes! The conversation with Bob and Lisa, dear friends you do not see nearly enough but when you do, it is always like this, always good conversation, always the easy time of people who have known each other for two decades, who have shared the gift of time.

Think of what you will, but at some point you will have to face the next evening, the choices that directed you toward your fate. Your legs were tired from having walked the snowy streets for hours, for two days, across the Seine and back, up the sloping sidewalk of Cardinal Lemoine to the many small shops of rue de Mouffetard, along Bd St-Germaine, stopping at cafés, random bookshops, stopping on the *riverain* to watch flake after flake melt in the Seine's icy mouth.

You decided to eat near the hotel that evening so that you could retire early, get an earlier start in the morning. You had a yen for more oysters but then you saw this cozy Italian restaurant named Caruso's and when you looked in you heard Caruso on the soundtrack singing *Pagliacci*, reminding you of the 78 rpm of Caruso your father had decades ago, and you thought a bit of pasta, a bit of Italian cheese, yes!

The waiter should have been warning enough— he spoke neither French nor English nor anything else it seemed, and the lack of communication did not concern him. You chose the spicy pasta. Somehow the waiter made you understand that it was *quite* spicy. *D'accord*, you said—did he think it was *too* spicy for you?—and tried to make him understand that you would have the platter of Italian cheeses afterwards and a *petit bouteille de vin rouge*. He brought everything at once and repeated to you that the pasta was spicy. Why did you not catch on that he was perhaps communicating something else, but from the depths of your own stupidity, by the time you had forked in four mouthfuls and it tasted like hell or worse, you decided subliminally that manhood and honor required you to eat some more. Halfway through you turned to the cheese but it was barely more edible, so you drank your barely potable wine and called for *l'addition, s'il vous plaît*!

It was but two blocks to the hotel but you stopped on rue de Rivoli at the Dôme to be served a couple of flutes of champagne by a woman tall and dark as your shadowy fantasies. She broke a glass on your table—a sign? You drank your champagne and, by way of entertainment, watched her move about the room, but halfway through the second glass, your stomach began to let you know that it was not finished with you for the evening, that things that would require your participation were beginning to happen.

In haste you paid and hastened back to the hotel, somehow

thought to snatch the Maxwell Kenton *Candy* and the Elkin book from the lobby shelves before lunging desperately up the four flights of stairs to your room—not possible to wait for the excruciatingly slow elevator *(Attention: This elevator is designed for two people or one person and a suitcase!)*

You made it to the room, threw off your coat and scarf and stood in the bathroom, over the great white telephone, peering at your puss in the mirror. Nothing happened. Your face was grey, more saggy than usual, but nothing happened. You stripped, slid into bed, cracked the Elkin, and read his essay about the worst thing he had ever done. He was at a writer's colony as the visiting writer. Somehow at this same colony there was also a visiting politician and on this particular occasion, just before the 1968 Chicago democratic convention, the visiting politician was Hubert H. Humphrey, far more celebrity than Elkin himself. Elkin carried his laundry up from the basement washroom and bumped into his hostess and Humphrey in the hall and the hostess introduced them and they shook hands. That evening, at a reception for Humphrey attended by a couple of hundred people, HHH hurried over when Elkin appeared to say, "I didn't know you were *that* Stanley Elkin!" For some reason Elkin felt patronized, and that annoyed him. A bit later, when Humphrey was surrounded by a deep broad semicircle of eager questioners—more like a press conference than a reception; after all, LBJ had stepped out of the race, Humphrey was the Democratic candidate—Elkin exacted his revenge. He had noticed on the table behind Humphrey a vat of cans of coca cola on ice, and during the pause of a silence between questions, Elkin said, "Mr. Humphrey, I have a question. Would you hand me a coca cola?" Everyone in the room fell still and Elkin made the great politician understand what he was asking him to do, and the great politician complied, reached behind him for a can of coke and forked it over, but Elkin was not finished. He asked, "Is that anyway to serve a coke! Unopened. I could cut my finger on the snaptop!"

By now you were laughing uncontrollably. Your eyes were tearing. Your laughter, in your own ears, sounded like weeping it was so high-pitched and frighteningly wild. You could not stop. You sounded like a lunatic. Alone in bed in Paris in a hotel room and cackling like someone in bedlam, weeping tears of insane merriment. What had come over you? Had you truly gone mad?

Then whatever it is that runs your body let you know what it required of you and you leapt to your feet and quickstepped into *le toilet* and stood again over that great white telephone, studying your blurred image in the little pool of water at its nadir. You opened your mouth. You gagged. Once. Twice. But your body was not releasing the poison that easily. Oh, no. Some lizard-like element within was telling you, This is *my* food and I am *keeping* it!

But greater forces were at play here—against the lizardy resistance Satanic powers reared up and with a mighty serpentine thrust of reverse peristalsis rippled the musculature of your trunk against the pouty greedy lizard and compelled him to release what he was holding on to.

*And*—as somebody or other used to sing in a Calypso melody— *you barfed. You barfed. Oh man, you should have seen me barf.*

You racketed from wall to wall. You gagged. You heaved. You barfed. You sagged to your knees and proverbially clung to the commode and looked into its hellish depths and you did not want to, did not want to look, but look you did, and the mere sight softened you to further release, and you called to god on the great white telephone but god was not home and you did not know his number and the operator had no cell listing and you kept barfing.

Then came respite of a sort. You stood like one of Francis Bacon's shitten dogs—yes, there was that too!—in the middle of the bathroom floor and peered into the mirror at yourself, and perhaps it was Stanley's influence, translating pity and fear into mockery and terror, but you could not fail to see the comic element in it all: there you stood, skin grey as your woolen scarf, dewlaps looking like dangling scraps of dark grey crepe paper, tears smeared around your bloodshot blue eyes, and your saggy mouth and droopy lips looking like some Jobian satire, pleading, "Why, god, *why?*"

You wiped your mouth with toilet paper—it might as well have been an asshole anyway. Wiped and tended to the parts rear and nether, washed, looked at your toothbrush and toothpaste with their promises of minty freshness, but then were advised by some primal instinct, joined in harmony with the warning voices of the translucent blue and pink toothbrush glasses, *not* to put that plastic brush into your face-hole unless you wanted to trigger another instantaneous bout of the gagging horrors.

You limped back to your bed and lay back upon it, picked up the Elkin and read on until Satan and the lizard began to duel again over what remained inside your miserable body and you were back in the torture chamber and Satan squeezed the lizard in both his mighty hands and the lizard opened its mouth—*your* mouth—and called *"O'Rourke!"* and on it went unto the wee hours: A quarter hour of Elkin, a quarter hour of horror, a moment of pity transforming in the mirror into comic self-mockery, and at one point peering at your reflection—old, dusty, worn-out—you realize truly that you are mortal, that you will die one day and that you will be glad to do it, that one day god in some way will say to you, *You've had enough old boy; I've decided that you are finished puking; you will never be required to puke again. Now take my hand and I shall bring you to nowhere for forever.*

And you will say, *Thank you, God. I sure did enjoy being here. Loved the sherbert and the dancing girls and the bubbly. Loved watching the snow on the Seine. Loved doing the two-backed beast once in a bit. Loved the champagne and the vodka—not to mention the literature. Oh god, yes, the literature! So very very glad to have been given this opportunity, but also so very very glad never to have to puke again. God? You are taking me now, right? Do you think you could say goodbye for me to all my colleagues and friends, all the people I love?*

But God says with a wise and not ungentle smile *No need for that, my boy; they will see that you are gone. Now take my hand and I shall lead you away. Over his shoulder he says, Bring out the bandoneon player!* And by god Edith Piaf is with him, singing in English: *Stranger beware zhere's love een zhe air/Under Paris skies...* And as God leads you by the hand, you see off in the vanishing point of nowhere that something great is waiting for you, something so wonderful and nullifying and as you get closer and closer it becomes dimmer and dimmer and the last words you hear echoing throughout eternity before the silence of forever are:

*Good grief—it's Mommy!*

# The Savor of Experience

*Gladys Swan*

It's a complicated business, the effort to locate the worst meal I've ever had. I can, for instance, remember a menu on a cruise ship to Bermuda that made your mouth water with expectation, only to bring you a piece of ham boiled to paleness that tasted like slightly flavored rubber bands. The cooks were English and apparently couldn't help themselves. But gradually, my thoughts about food and the meals I've eaten have wandered into various byways of consideration—not forgetting the food itself or personal likes and dislikes. Serve up a plate of buttered beets to my husband, and he'd run for the nearest exit. I can think of certain tastes I developed as I grew up. By the time I was ten I'd developed a continuing taste for oysters on the half shell—problematic to a good many palates; I ate without complaint the tongue and liver my mother prepared, foods I now tend to avoid. The food itself is only part of the equation—it goes without saying. Good meals appear in the most unlikely spots, and bad ones can be shamelessly presented on elegant tables.

Meals were not a source of pleasure in our household. My father brought home the frustrations of his business day, while my mother, home cooking, had time to work up her own set over the stove. Despite all her efforts to please, my father would often push away his plate, the food scarcely touched. It wasn't to his taste; his stomach bothered him; he would eat something later. Meanwhile the radio served up World War II, and it was at one's peril to dare to interrupt H.V. Kaltenborn.

Some years later, in *The Odyssey,* "that great book of eating," as Fielding called it, I discovered other approaches to food, the spectrum of possibilities ranging from the barbaric to the highly civilized. In contrast to the cannibalism of the Cyclops and the excesses and wantonness of the suitors, hospitality emerged as an ideal. The stranger was received with courtesy, bathed, given fresh clothing, then offered food and wine, without even revealing his name. First his needs as a human being had to be satisfied, and then in the context of ritual and sacrifice the group came to together as a community. A feast at Nestor's palace. The reception at Nausicaa's. Lord and Lady Menelaus graciously entertaining at home.

This was fine for literature—inspiring to think about. I had no real expectation of encountering that sort of joyful participation, that communion between host and guest in the so-called real world—until one Sunday afternoon in Indiana. My husband and I were invited to dinner at the home of Luigi, a painter and sculptor, who had come to teach art at the small liberal arts college where we both taught. His wife, Dorothy, an American, who had lived with him for a number of years in Italy, had inherited a cabin down in Brown Country, where they were currently living. A warm and cozy place. They were fixing it up.

Soon after we arrived and were enjoying a glass of wine, two cousins, Belle and Clara, dropped in. Dorothy was delighted—she hadn't seen them for quite a while. Then a young couple new in the neighborhood came by to visit. Dorothy invited them to stay for supper. Too bad Charlie wasn't there. Why not see if he could come. He could and did, another cousin—a diffident man in his late fifties, who was greeted with enthusiasm. "Charlie is the sweetest kisser," Clara announced. "Yes, you are," she insisted when he demurred. "Isn't he, Belle? Come— Give me a kiss, Charlie." She stood up. After a slight hesitation, he obliged. "There, just like I remember." Another glass or two of wine and I'd have been tempted to try him myself.

44

So there we were, nine people for dinner, mostly strangers to one another.

But not for long. After the first tentative efforts toward conversation, the exchange grew lively. We became intensely interested in one another as the talk flowed with the wine. Everyone had a story to tell. I remember that the sisters' lives had been changed by their friendship with a neighbor, Mr. Clausen, who owned a 1927 Cadillac. "We used to go over to watch him polish his beautiful car and sometimes he took us for rides. Such a thrill." And when he died, they discovered that they had inherited, not only the car and a whole set of spare parts, but a life that opened outward from it. For years they were invited to be in parades of old cars, at times to lead the whole procession. They wore Twenties outfits. "We had a ball."

At one point, I wandered out to the kitchen to see if Dorothy needed any help. No, but I could sit and chat with her. What fascinated me was the manner of her preparations, an attitude that was new to me. She handled each lettuce leaf as though it was a thing of value, to be appreciated. Her face, her absorption and delight in what she was doing, gave a light to the room. I felt as though I'd entered some kind of enchantment, where each thing revealed a hidden life. Food was more than something to eat. Everything came together in the pleasure, first of the company, then the meal— all of us there joined by a kind of intimacy. A meal of spaghetti and salad, bread and wine. Simple enough, but all one needed.

Except for our hosts, I never saw any of these people again. A group of strangers come together by chance had been held for a moment in a kind of creative eros and then dispersed. But the whole experience left me something to savor—something I hoped for when people came together to share a meal. Something that included and went beyond the pleasure of the food.

But food can be subject to a variety of influences. Recently when I was traveling in Ecuador, my companion and I, in the mood for Italian food one evening, chose a place called the Roma. We walked into a dining area crammed with paintings. Even the surfaces of the tables were painted scenes. Drama, sentiment and searing color leapt from the walls: the huge head of a maddened bull; two scantily clad dancers in a serpentine pose, with limbs as pliable as spaghetti; Mary and the baby Jesus, their expressions more self-satisfied than tender, with bits of stone and glass decorating haloes and headdresses, collars and wrists; a man, woman and child, bathed in a garish red glow looking toward a volcano; two gladiators, one on the ground, the other standing—both covered with bloody gashes. A couple of landscapes approached the mediocre.

Apart from our being the only diners in the restaurant, I should have immediately given way to my misgivings. What sort of feeling for food could be fostered in such surroundings? The lasagna came in an aluminum foil container, probably frozen, then heated in a microwave, instead of being a square cut from a dish someone there had actually cooked.. It was mostly a pile of ground meat with cheese melted on top, with nothing resembling a lasagna noodle. The ravioli I ordered was of the toughest dough I've ever encountered. Very small lumps of spinach with tiny specks of ricotta formed the centers. After the first bite or two I could think only of what might be happening to my stomach. We knew only one thing to do—to pay the bill as quickly as possible and head off for something edible. At least we were free to do that.

But for the worst meal I have ever eaten, I would have to return to Greece.

At the time I was traveling with a Dutch friend, Louisa, who had made seventeen trips to Greece and spoke the language fluently. This gave her a real advantage, and certain privileges. She liked to go to the tavernas and sit and joke with the men, who, if at first taken aback, were amused by her boldness and seemed to enjoy her presence. She was, after all, a foreigner and therefore allowed to enter precincts where a Greek woman did not intrude.

One day a woman Louisa knew from previous visits, Katerina,

begged her to tell her husband to come home. He practically lived in the taverna and she hadn't seen him for days. Louisa, not wanting to be caught in the middle of a domestic imbroglio, gently declined to be the messenger. Finally, the woman herself was desperate enough to enter the taverna and confront her husband. Incensed, he told her to get out, and the two of them shouted at one another until the proprietor made her leave.

Because of her connection with Louisa, she invited us to dinner. She was a woman in her sixties, dressed typically in black. We found her alone. The interior of her house, dimly lit, was covered with icons of saints and photos of various relatives. Heavy dark furniture filled the living room, and cabinets of dishes lined the walls of the dining room. The bare spaces were filled with shelves of knickknacks.

I was introduced to Katerina, who lost interest in my presence after we'd both exhausted what few Greek or English expressions we knew. Louisa was our intermediary, but clearly she was there to listen. And though I couldn't understand until afterwards what Katerina was saying, I could recognize anger and complaint. She spent her days taking care of the house, doing the washing and the cooking, and did her husband come even to eat the food she'd prepared? No, he was always with his cronies, coming home at all hours, staggering drunk, hardly speaking to her, just flopping into bed. And gone again the next day. Some nights he didn't come home at all. What was he doing all that time? And hadn't she been a good wife to him? Meanwhile, almost stifled, I tried to think of how the rooms would look if everything was cleared out--all the stuff on the shelves swept away, and the heavy furniture thrown in the dump. I could imagine space and air.

Finally, her litany given out, Katerina served the meal. A cold meal of small fish that had been cooked perhaps a day or several days before for the husband who refused to come home. I remember the fish as being stiff, with sharp fins, as though they could have stood on their own. Unpalatable  There were cold potatoes and beans that appeared to be leftovers as well. It may have been the best she could offer. What did her husband leave her to spend on food? What delight could she take in preparing it?

At one point, as I was trying to get past the fish bones, Katherina looked out the front window. "There goes my daughter-in-law," she said. "She doesn't come to see me anymore. She's not even looking this way." Indeed the woman strode past, her eyes fixed on what was ahead of her.

Finally it was over. We had eaten as much as we could manage and stayed long enough to fulfill the role of guests. I noticed that Katerina herself had eaten practically nothing. With great relief we escaped into the evening. The sound of the sea and the scent of lemons were in the air. The sky was filled with stars. Louisa and I walked in silence for a time. Then Louisa gave a little laugh of chagrin. Nothing to be done about it. The unfortunate woman had lived out her domestic role, and for whatever reasons, had been left to marinate in her bitterness until she was hardly fit for human companionship. The celebrated Greek hospitality had shriveled with her.

This was the time when a group of women in Athens opened up a coffee house, a place just for women to come and socialize. The police closed them down after a few weeks on some pretext, and they were fighting to re-open. I never knew the outcome.

Whatever the food, I would say now, a meal offers the savor of experience: the culture, the social mores, the personal sensibility of the cook and the one who holds the fork or chopsticks are always there subtly or not so subtly influencing every bite—in our daily search for nourishment.

# Sneeze Dressing & Caribou Gravy

*Duff Brenna*

January 2003. Yukon. Whitehorse International Airport. The temperature is five to six below zero. Ricki and I are sitting in a Douglas DC-3, circa WWII. We are two of thirty-two passengers. The plane is so cold it's as if we're sitting in the middle of an ice cube. We're dressed for survival. Long underwear and layered shirts and sweaters and jeans. Three pairs of woolly socks on our feet tucked into Ice Fields snow boots. I'm sitting next to a port side window and can see the propeller turning wearily, like a windmill in a timid breeze. "Is it too cold to start?" Ricki asks. "No way," I tell her (as if I know what I'm talking about)."This is par for the course. Nothing to it," I say.

The DC-3 doesn't make a liar of me. With a sudden burst of fiery flatulence and billowing smoke the engine catches and the propeller becomes a whirling blur. The right side engine goes through the same motions before it, too, coughs into life. It takes another twenty minutes before the engines start feeding the heating system warm air. Ten to fifteen minutes later we're almost cozy. Cozy enough to take off our hats and gloves.

The plane taxis to the runway. Ricki takes my hand and squeezes it so hard she's actually hurting me. She doesn't like airplanes at all. She especially doesn't like the old prop-driven types. She wants jet engines at the very least. But it's mid-winter and if we're going to travel above the Arctic Circle, this old plane is our only option. The plane picks up speed, goes faster (furiously faster), its torque an invisible hand thrusting us deep into our seats. In seconds we're climbing toward feathery cirrus clouds. Below are stark-naked hardwoods, their arms black in the struggling light of morning. Miles of evergreens huddling together. Cabins dotting the scenery. Smoke-spewing from chimneys. Snow and more snow. Lakes and ponds covered in milky ice.

We're on our way to The Northwest Territories, to Inuvik (place of man), population 3,000, fifty miles south of the Arctic Ocean. North of Inuvik is the hamlet called Tuktoyaktuk (stone caribou), commonly called Tuk, home to approximately 900 people living at the edge of the ocean itself. We're not going to Tuk. We've reserved a four-wheeler and plan to drive the ice road to a place called Aklavik (place of grizzly), a village of 594 people bordering the Peel Channel of the Mackenzie River, the longest river in Canada.

I've been living in a cabin ten miles outside of Whitehorse (population 20,000) since November 2002, using the city's library to do research for a novel I'm writing called *The Willow Man*. Which was prompted by reading a book by Dick North called *The Mad Trapper of Rat River*. North's book is a factual account of the hunt for Albert Johnson in the winter of 1931-32. Johnson shot a Canadian policeman who was attempting to question him about allegations made by local trappers who said Johnson had been tampering with their traps and stealing their game. The largest manhunt in the history of The Northwest Territories ensued. It took nearly two months before the posse was able to track Johnson down. He wouldn't surrender. He shot it out with his pursuers for nearly an hour before a bullet pierced his spleen, gut, liver and killed him.

*The Willow Man* is based on the hunt for Johnson, only in my fictional account, my main character, Triple E, is alone in the winter mountains trying to find Johnson. Johnson was from Aklavik. He's buried there. I want to visit the village to give my novel that stamp of authenticity it needs to have when I write about the area. Ricki, my adventurous soulmate, has flown to Whitehorse in order to go with me and help me in whatever way she can.

Our first landing is in Dawson, Jack London's old stomping grounds when he went to the Yukon during the gold rush. London didn't get rich from his diggings, but he found plenty of riches to write about: *The Call of the Wild, White Fang*, numerous short stories. I'm hoping that what inspired him will inspire me too.

Half of the passengers disembark in Dawson. Again we roar down a runway and climb into the skies. Fifty minutes later we land in Old Crow, population 260. There are no cars in Old Crow. No way to get there but by plane or sled dogs or snowmobiles. Several snowmobiles arrive and the natives unload supplies from the belly of the plane. Steamy houses (hardly more than huts) fan out from the airport. Every roof has a pipe spewing smoke. Old Crow natives hunt and fish, largely living off what are called Porcupine caribou. With the occasional moose, deer, char, trout and whatever small animals they might snare. Here and there, incongruously, I note satellite TV antennas. I've read about Old Crow in the Whitehorse Library. There is no liquor allowed in Old Crow, but some of those who live there manage to get it anyway. Teenagers, the young and restless, have booze parties. Like teenagers everywhere, they get drunk and make fools of themselves, and of course their parents lament about how the younger generation is going to hell. Whitehorse has the same problem.

No one gets off the plane in Old Crow. No one gets on. Next stop Inuvik.

When we disembark and go inside the terminal, the first thing we see is a ten foot polar bear standing on its hind legs, black claws out as if about to grab us. Mouth open, great canines bared, ready to bite. "Hope we don't see any of those," Ricki tells me. "They generally stay farther north up above Tuk," I answer. "Pregnant females are hibernating, so at least that cuts down the chances of meeting some of them." "Sleep, mama polar bear, sleep," she says laughing the laugh I love, full of Ricki's high spirits. "Do you think we'll see the northern lights, the Aurora Borealis?" she wonders. "Good chance of it," I tell her. "I sooo want to see those lights!" she says.

We rent a Chevy Yukon and drive into town. It's already twilight and the moon hangs low and full in the sky. Smoke and steam rise from businesses and houses reminding me of Old Crow. All the buildings are built on gravel and pilings so they won't sink into the permafrost. We stop at the PIZZA HUT and eat a rather stale (perhaps old frozen?) pepperoni pizza for dinner. Then we leave and find POLAR BED & BREAKFAST—"Open Year Round Baths Phone Cable TV." We rent a room for two nights. The B & B is far from fancy. The rooms are small, holding a double bed, a nightstand and a lamp. There are a couch and two easy chairs in the living room. A TV. We watch *JOHN STEWART's DAILY SHOW*. Get some laughs. Go to bed early.

It's still dark when we rise the next morning. The kitchen is more like a wide hallway with cupboards and a counter. The breakfast is cereal: Fruit Loops or Cheerios or Corn Flakes. There is milk in the tiny refrigerator. But make your own coffee, pilgrim.

By nine a.m. faint light is washing the southeast sky. Enough to see where we're going. I drive us down to River Road and plunge the SUV over the side, sliding it down the embankment and onto the Mackenzie. Next to me Ricki gasps and giggles, but doesn't say anything.

The ice is as smooth as it would be inside an ice rink. Pickup trucks with huge drills attached to their heavy back bumpers are drilling holes, pumping up water that will freeze and thicken. Right now the ice is twelve to thirteen inches thick. When the drillers are finished it will be sixteen inches or more and able to hold a semi loaded with food and other supplies for Tuk, which only gets its supplies from the air now. I have a map of the river and its various tributaries, one of which will lead us to the Peel River channel and Aklavik.

I find the main offshoot I want. At least I think it's the one I want. In any case, it's going the right direction. Going southwest. I do want to go southwest, don't I? Then west. Then northwest. That's what the map shows me.

Sometimes the wheels seem to float. I ease the steering a little this way or that way and nothing happens for a second or two. And then, lazily, the SUV responds. There are numerous branches of the river that twist, meander, fold back on the main Mackenzie. Across some stretches there is enough sticky snow to give the tires better traction. But they keep breaking loose, drifting at odd angles, especially on the tighter river turns, a whoop sensation in the rear end that would be fun if it were a carnival ride. I stay off the brakes and use the SUV's gears to slow down. If we really started skating, we might loop the loop all the way to one embankment or the other, where there are frozen logs, hummocks of snow and ice-jams that could catch us, flip the Chevy like a coin. The course of the river runs south at times, but sometimes on a shortcut we are going north, sometimes east, often southwest, which is the way I want to go. Or do I? There are dozens of feeders, some nearly as wide as the main Mackenzie itself and tempting to take. But taking any of them might get us going in circles, lost in a maze.

Ricki keeps asking me, "Is this the way? Are you sure? Are you sure this ice is safe? What about those cracks I keep seeing?" "No problem, no problem," I assure her.

When the sun at noon is a fiery, half-buried wheel on the southern horizon, I stop and we sit on the ice listening to the wind chewing the windows. The engine shakes as if it's cold and impatient to go. "Are we lost?" Ricki asks. "Look how beautiful it is," I tell her. The half-disk of the rolling sun south of us spreads orange-pink ribbons across the landscape. The snow is piled in places like pink cotton candy. Orange flames seem to come from under the ice. As if there's a fire below. Like water is fire. Pink mist moves in tiny tornadoes swirling over the ice. Along both banks spindly stands of Black Spruce resemble shrimp-pink torches. "It's a weird other world," I say. "Never seen anything like it. Like something from Picasso or Dali. Or maybe Sigmund Freud." Ricki wants to get moving again. She says the ice we're on has never been traveled before. She calls it virgin ice.

I drive for who knows how many miles before I realize I no longer have any idea where the tributary leading to Aklavik is. "I think we've gone too far," I say. The gas tank is less than half full. I'm pretty sure I can find my way back to Inuvik. But I want to go to Aklavik. I came to this frozen land to find Aklavik. I'm not turning around until I find the damn place. Which way? Which way?

While I'm trying to decide what to do, I spot a small white pickup coming towards us. A human being! I stop the Chevy, jump out and wave my hands. A grizzled man of perhaps sixty stops and rolls down his window. What doin? he says, voice gravely, a little annoyed. "Trying to find Aklavik," I tell him. "Wrong way," he says. "Back six clicks. Go west at the overturned canoe. Northwest when the channel ends." I thank him and without another word my grumpy guardian angel appearing (it seems) out of nowhere, drives on. I turn the four-wheeler around and we find the overturned canoe and the narrow tributary leading to Aklavik.

There is only one gas station/convenience store in town. It's painted bright red and stands out against the snowy white roads and houses. When the station attendant starts filling my tank he says, "How you get here, ey?" I tell him the ice road. And he tells me the ice road to Tuk is open, but the one to Aklavik is closed. No one is supposed to drive on it until it's graded and tested. It's an $800 fine if I'm caught. He tells me to watch for black helicopters. "Thems the ones." I go in the store and buy some smoked salmon and crackers and cheese and a big bottle of Coke. I ask the clerk about Albert Johnson's grave and he tells me no one can get to the graveyard right now, it's piled with several feet of snow. Come back next summer. Take the ferry.

*Why didn't I think of that?* I ask myself. Snow piled everywhere and yet it never crossed my mind that I wouldn't be able to visit the dead desperado's grave and drive all over Aklavik and take pictures and talk to people out and about. No one is out and about. They've all got more sense than to be out and about. Wind is full of razors. Snow is swirling. The temperature is zero. My heart sinks. All this way and nothing to show for it but surreal scenery. Goodbye Albert Johnson. Rest In Peace, you rotten son of a ...

We snack a little as I drive us back to the very narrow tributary leading to the main river. I pick at the salmon a bit. Ricki sips Coke. Says she can't eat a thing. The wind is blowing harder and my stomach is churning. Snow drifts are piling up, hindering us. Time and again I have to plow the Yukon through drift after drift praying we don't get stuck. If we did and night came on and the gas ran out—don't go there! Ricki never says a word about what we're both thinking.

It's nearly dark by the time we get to the wide channel leading to the main branch that leads northeast to Inuvik. As we enter the smooth ice again we pass a plywood sign to our left that says ROAD CLOSED!!! "I didn't notice that before, did you?" I ask. She shakes her head no. And not five minutes later, a black helicopter whips over us. "There it is," I say. "What do you mean?"she says. So I tell her we've been illegal all day. The Aklavik road wasn't actually open. We could have been arrested and fined. But it all worked out, so what the hell. The helicopter didn't see us until we were well beyond the warning sign.

Ricki says, "You're kidding, you're kidding!" Her gray-green eyes are as wide and shiny as quarters. "Arrested," she murmurs.

"Look, everything's okay, honey. Listen, I tell you what we're going to do. I'm taking you to the best restaurant in town and we're going to have the best meal in Inuvik. I don't care what it costs, you order anything you want. New York steak, baked potato, salad, the works. Whaddaya say, sweetheart?" "Arrested." is what she says. "Arrested."

I take her to a nice looking Restaurant/Hotel called The MacKENZIE "Inuvik's Frontier Hotel. Green Briar Dining Room: Superb Food Featuring Northern and Canadian cuisine." I pull into the parking lot and am grateful to see plug-in engine heaters. And I'm thinking *that's thoughtful.* We can have a great dinner and when we come back our engine will still be warm. What a great place. We go inside and take off our coats, hats, gloves and sit at a table and order double vodka martinis. We look at the menu. "I'm so hungry I could eat a moose," I say. I savor my martini. Ah, yes, this is life. This is living.

The manager comes to our table and I'm thinking he's going to welcome us. Ask us if we like our martinis. Yeah, I'm thinking he'll say something like, Where you from, folks? That sort of nice proprietor stuff is what I'm expecting to hear. I'm smiling at him in anticipation as he says, "You got a room here?" "No room, no room, just here for dinner," I answer. And he says gruffly, "Engine heaters for them's got rooms. Not allowed to plug in, not without you got a room" "Well," I reply, "I had no idea. I thought those plug-ins were a courtesy." "Nope, you gotta have a room." "So you want me to go unplug my engine, huh?" "Actually, it don't matter," he says, a belligerent look in his eyes. "Electricity ain't even on out there."

Now, I'm an even-tempered guy. Years of practice have taught me to hold back what used to be an explosive temper, but this motherfucker has tripped a switch. "Then what the hell you even bring it up for?" I say. "Why say a fuckin word if it don't matter, man? What the hell's your fucking problem? You think we're eating here? Not a fucking chance, Jack." I gesture to Ricki, "C'mon, we're fuckin outta here! Jesus, how stupid can you get!" I throw a Canadian ten on the table. We grab our gear and leave. "If he follows me or says another word, I'll punch his lights out!" I snarl. Goddamn I'm mad. I'm mad and tired and I want another goddamn martini! I unplug the engine and we sizzle tires getting out of there. Drive not far, just a few blocks to a place called ESKIMO INN. "In House Dining, Caribou Dining Room Featuring Caribou Steaks, Arctic Char as well as a Full Range of Western and European Dishes."

"Okay, this sounds good," say I, trying to calm down, trying to recover my equilibrium, my celebratory mood.

A stringy-haired waitress sits us at a table and hands out menus. "Two vodka martinis," I say. And she says no martinis. She can give us wine or beer. No martinis in the dining room. Have to drink martinis in the bar. "Wine it is then. Bring us a carafe of the house red." Which she does and it tastes like ... well, it tastes like Pisano, only more sour than peppery. No matter. It'll be fine with food. I order a New York steak medium rare. Adventurous Ricki wants to try that caribou. It's been an adventurous day, why not caribou? Hell yes caribou it is. I order salad with blue cheese dressing. Waitress shakes her head. There are no salad fixings. Green beans come with the meals. Green beans it is then. No problem. I'm famished.

We wait. And we wait. Until finally the waitress brings our food. She sets my plate in front of me and—ABRUPTLY-STARTINGLY—sneezes. "Oh, excuse me," she says. "So sorry." "It's okay, no problem," I tell her. I look at my New York and find it covered with dark brown gelatinous gravy. And instead of sour cream and chives and butter for my baked potato, I find it is also slathered with the same dark brown gelatinous gravy. I look at Ricki's plate, and, yep, same thing, brown gravy. "How's the caribou?" I ask her. She takes a bite. Grimaces, "Ugh, what's this awful texture?" she says. I put a bite in my mouth. Chew. And tell her it's liver. Or at least it's got the crumbly rubbery texture of liver. Ricki picks at her potato, but she doesn't like it either. I try to eat my New York and find it's as chewy as beef jerky. I try what looks to be an oven-baked potato, but I can't stand that damn gravy. I scrape it off, but still taste gravy as soon as I put a bite of potato in my mouth. And the green beans? Forget it.

I call the stringy-haired waitress over and tell her we can't eat our dinners. She chews her lips. She sniffs noisily. Wipes her runny nose with the butt of her hand. And tells us she's sorry. She says the cook back there is the dishwasher filling in for the real cook who is off with the flu. She thinks she might have the flu too. She glances at her boss sitting on a stool behind the cash register reading a magazine. "I'm sorry," she says. "You still have to pay for it," she says. "He'll call the police if you don't. I can wrap it up for you." I wave off that idea. She hands me a bill for a hundred and twenty-three Canadian dollars. What can I do? I throw the money on the table (no tip) and we walk out blinking our eyes with incredulity and LAUGHING. We go to the liquor store (only one in Inuvik) and buy a bottle of Iceberg Vodka.

Back at the B & B, we kick back on the couch, drinking our vodka, eating our salmon and cheese and crackers. We end up hooting ourselves half sick about the day we've had: Lost on the Mackenzie, slipping and sliding, low on gas, cracks in the ice, snowbound Aklavik, no Albert Johnson, fierce winds creating drifts threatening to bury us, helicopter buzzing us, $800 fine if he had caught us five minutes earlier. Ah, but the fine feast waiting for us! What a sweet man that manager was! I think we might skip eating there tomorrow. And also skip the ESKIMO INN and the flu sneezy waitress and that godawful gravy! Pour me another vod, baby. At least the ice road was fun, ey?

She tells me that she was never so terrified in her life. That ice river road almost made her pee her pants. "Why didn't you say something?" I ask her. "No way. I wasn't going to ruin things for you or have you take me back. If the ice broke, I was going down with you." "I'd never put you in that kind of danger," I tell her. "I drove all over frozen lakes when I was a kid in Minnesota. There's no danger. You think those pickups would have been out there if there was any danger?" "Duff," she says, "the sign read ROAD CLOSED!" "Well,

58

that's true enough, I guess. But really, the only danger we were in is that we might get lost and run out of gas. That ice wouldn't break in a million years." "Famous last words,? she says. We raise our glasses and drink to that.

Later that night just before bedtime I look out the window and see an Irish Green Scarf hanging miles high in the atmosphere. We bundle up and hurry outside and there they are: gorgeous emerald lights filling the sky. "We saw them!" Ricki says. "The northern lights, we saw them!"

"A good omen," I tell her.

# Danish Xmas Lunch

## *Dennys Khomate*

Here's the deal. All year I've been working in this office. It is an office that does good work, humanitarian even. There are men and women who work in this office, mostly Danes. Fortunately for me, because I am a man, there are more women than men working here. The men and women have dealings with one another every day. Unlike our wives (if you're reading this, honey, this is only hypothetical), these women are on their best behavior with us, and unlike their mates, we are on our best behavior with them. We tolerate small annoyances and do not flare up at one another. We do not nag and bitch in the office. That sort of behavior is reserved for the home front. We smile at one another as we pass in the hallway— as opposed to the sneering grunts that are occasionally exchanged at home (but never with you, hon!) I glance back over my shoulder and see that most of these women in the office look as good going as they do coming. Sometimes they glance back at me, too, and catch me glancing back at them, and we each smile with guilty pleasure.

We appreciate one another and develop lots of secret crushes. Unless you have only been married for a very few years, it is difficult to still have a crush on your mate (the case of my wife and me, of course, is an exception—right, honey?), and you wonder why your wife or husband cannot be as sweet and agreeable as the people in the office.

As a result, the pressure of these crushes leads to erotic speculation which builds up over the year, but now it is December, and there is going to be a Christmas lunch for all hundred some odd employees in the main dining room of the 200-year-old villa in which our humanitarian organization is located. This Christmas lunch is a fringe benefit. It is also a pressure valve that will allow everyone to let off some of their secret steamy thoughts.

This year someone has devised a seating plan. I am grateful for that because various means have been used in the past to figure out who is to sit together at the tables with as even as possible a distribution of men and women. In past years, this has been done by having people choose from a system of colored ribbons, of numbered tickets, of color-coded pictures of fruits or flowers. For example, all men who chose a blue banana and all women who chose a pink banana got to sit at the table designated the banana table. Another year, each man placed his right shoe in an enormous burlap sack, and each woman picked out a shoe and had to find the man who belonged to that shoe as her table mate. This resulted in a great deal of confusion because a lot of men had the same kind of shoes.

Last year was absolutely the worst I ever experienced in this regard. Each year one department is responsible for the organization of the Christmas lunch, and last year it was organized by the Nasty Bitch Department. The supervisor of the Nasty Bitch department, let's call her Ms. NB, decided to make a feminist sex-object point by having each of the men pick two stickered place numbers and then pull up his pants legs to above the knee and place the numbered stickers on each knee. The men then had to stand behind a screen that masked them down to their bare knees and kick their legs as on a chorus line while the women paraded past on the other side of the screen to decide which legs appealed to them for a table mate whereupon they plucked the number sticker from the right knee of their choice, then came around and claimed the man with the corresponding number on his left knee.

It had never occurred to me until that moment that I might have unattractive knees, but I was the next to last of the fifty or so men whose number was selected. Which I have to admit did teach me something about the potential for humiliation in being looked upon as a sex object.

This year is different, however. I find my place at one of the thirteen tables of eight. My table has five women and three men—an auspicious start. I am placed between a woman from the Finance Department named Dorthe whose profound intention to have fun is clearly exhibited in the depth of her cleavage and, unfortunately, Ms. NB from the NB Department who embraces me from behind, cups her hands over my pectorals and says, "Hhhmmm.... I'm guessing a B cup."

"You, madame," I retort, "are not a gentleman!"

"My intentions have never been that low," she responds with a smirk, and it occurs to me that I might be in for a rough riding this year after all.

Across the table from me, however, I am pleased to note, is Sascha from the Service Department upon whom I have a crush and who is built rather like Birgitte Stallone née Nielsen and is clearly proud of the valley of her pulchritude. I successfully resist telling my anecdote of Hamilton Jordan in the White House who once remarked to the Egyptian Ambassador's wife, wearing low décolletage, "I have always longed to see your pyramids."

I am further pleased to note the fact that the table is set with beer and schnapps glasses, that this is going to be a true Danish lunch—hard core. There is a round of introductions; in addition to Sascha, Dorthe and Ms NB, there is Ruth from Finance with her sexy mouth (what was God thinking to give such a sexy mouth to an accountant?!), and Viveca from personnel with wondrous hips and slender waist and sparkling eyes, young Alan from the Repro Unit (joke potential there), bearded Martin, also from Finance, and myself, Assistant Director of the Ethics Unit.

Having formally shaken hands, we proceed to the buffet line. I am happy to be behind Sascha who turns to me and exclaims, "Doesn't it look delicious?!" I survey the many kinds of herring (pickled, curried, fried, sherried), salmon, breaded warmed plaice filets, smoked eel with scrambled egg and chives, cod roe with capers and mayonnaise, caviar with onion and lemon, then I glance into the vale of Sascha's beauties.

"And so nicely displayed," I agree.

She slaps my arm and says, "You're so silly!"

"Silly bad or silly good?"

"Silly bad," she says, leaning into my face.

"Bad bad or good bad?"

"Take some food," she urges, and I do so, realizing that I might be off to a bad start—a bad-bad start—but with all this cleavage all around me, I have begun to wonder whether my marriage will survive this day. The wife will know, of course. As soon as I get home, she will look at my face and printed there will be a most legible list of all transgressions I commit during the course of the next ten hours, and she will read straight down that list with increasingly bitter fury. Of course, next week will be *her* Xmas lunch, but she has better self-control and is more mature than I. Or is she? Maybe she's just better at hiding her transgressions.

It occurs to me that I should concentrate on the here and now, and now we are back here at our table, and our schnapps glasses have been filled to convexity, and opened bottles of Tuborg Xmas Beer (5.8% alcoholic content) are beside our beautifully tapered beer glasses, steaming cold, and many additional bottles of Xmas Beer are clustered about the table along with two full liters of icy Krone schnapps.

Now that food and drink are within reach, we turn formal. Conversation stops. Each person in the room concentrates on spreading fat on a slice of dark rye bread. The fat is in little packets marked with the brand name, *Bedstemors Fedt*, which literally translates as "Grandmother's Fat."

"Whose grandmother?" I wonder, and Ms. NB gazes icily at me. "Pig," she intones.

64

Then atop the grandmother fat we place a filet or two of pickled herring, atop that, working skillfully with knife and fork, rings of raw onion and capers. We slice a morsel of this delicacy, fork it to our tongues, chew, swallow, lift the schnapps glass and present it, look by turn into the eyes of each person sitting around the table, sip, sigh, look again into the eyes of each person while once again presenting the glass, set the glass down. Then it is every man for himself. Conversation resumes. Cheeks bulge with food, teeth munch, throats bob with swallowing, and the sound level in the room begins to rise until the company director, a Swede named Elsnab, clinks his glass with the tines of his fork, and all fall silent.

Elsnab rises and begins to sing a song about the eel on our plates. The main characters of the song are the baby eels who alert Eel Mama to the fact that Eel Papa is in danger. By turns, from verse to verse, they alert her to the fact that Eel Papa is looking at a worm on a hook, that Eel Papa is eating the worm, that Eel Papa has been hooked, is being drawn up toward the surface of the sea... To each observation from the baby eels, Eel Mama reassures them not to worry, that Eel Papa will be coming back again, and with each reassurance, there is a chorus of voices in the room shouting, "Skål!" whereupon everyone lifts his schnapps glass and sips heftily. Finally, the baby eels advise Eel Mama that Eel Papa has been pulled out of the water, skinned and sliced and placed in a frying pan over the fire. Then the song turns somber as Eel Mama informs the children, "Eel Papa will never come back again." And then there is a mournful verse, followed by a chorus of "Skål!" and the drinking of schnapps and refilling of schnapps glasses.

By now everyone, except those few drinking Fanta instead of beer and schnapps (i.e. Ms. NB) is drunk. Throughout the singing, I have been regularly looking into the blue blue sparkling eyes of Sascha who has been returning my gaze with undeniable fondness from across the table, and I find myself falling deeply in love, and the display of her breasts is so magnificent that I have been inspired to begin to serenade her with a slowed-down version of a classic ethnic American love song with its piquant lines:  I can't believe my eyes that all belongs to you and *I'm like a one-eyed cat, peekin' in a sea-food store and Go over the hill and way down underneath...* The excellent and deeply romantic nature of these lines has never fully occurred to me before.  Apparently, they have also occurred to Ms. NB on my left who demands to know precisely what I mean by "way down underneath." Martin from the Finance Department, whose beard is peppered with bits of chive and who is a great reader, tells her it is a reference to the writings of E. Hemingway who penned the famous line, "A bitch is a bitch is a bitch."

Remaining cool, Ms. NB advises Martin that he can expect to be cited for sexual chicanery come Monday.  Meanwhile Alan from the Repro Unit is serenading the sexy mouth of Ruth from Finance with a verse of "Come Home to Aarhus," and Viveca from Personnel with her wondrous hips and slender waist is standing up on the seat of her chair to prove that she is able to do so and urging us all to prove that we can, too, and we do that, all except for Ms. NB who pronounces us all ridiculous and pathetic and storms off to smoke a cigarette in the smoking corner.

We balance there on our chair seats, feeling ridiculous and pathetic, fresh bottles of Xmas Brew held aloft and swaying in time to the song we sing in chorus, lyrics by the beloved Danish poet Benny Andersen which goes:

Life is not the worst thing we have
And soon the coffee is ready.
My wife comes naked from the bath,
While I eat a cheese sandwich...

As always happens at about this point in the office's annual Danish Xmas lunch, I begin to lose my sense of time and continuity and develop a certain degree of tunnel vision.  Pinpoint scraps of experience stand out.  At one moment, I find myself standing *en embrace* with Sascha in the library whispering about how much I wish to place my lips in her cleavage which she allows me to do. At the next moment, I seem to be walking toward the smoking corner and feeling sorry for Ms NB who is sitting all alone puffing on a cigarette; I ask if she has the Xmas blues, and she responds in Danish idiom that I should *scram straight into hell!*

Then I find myself in an armchair enjoying a deep snifter of cognac and a Flora Danica cigar and next moment dancing a conga line around the Christmas tree down in the lobby then back on the queue for coffee and cognac, falling in love with the gorgeous plump rump of the woman ahead of me on line and unsuccessfully resisting the urge to tell her so, expecting a slap, but being rewarded with a smile and the thrusting backward of her treasure to be admired.

God, I love this country!

Then I am in the darkened library again, playing dueling banjoes with our tongues with Sascha and she whispers that she would like me to do to her something I have never even tried with my wife and am not certain I am physically capable of, at least at this moment.

Then, mysteriously, I am out the back door of our building and on the cold dark avenue, wearing my overcoat and scarf and hat and gloves and unable to get a taxi cab. No one is ever able to get a taxi cab in Copenhagen on a Xmas lunch Friday in December. My apartment is only three miles away so I decide that a walk in the cold air will do me good. Actually the distance is increased beyond three miles because everyone knows the shortest distance between two points is a straight line, but my feet are insisting on covering the pavement in a zigzag pattern. I am aware that this is making more work for me, but my feet seem to be enjoying the zigzags and refuse to stop.

By midnight or somewhat thereafter, I am home. The apartment is dark. In the bathroom, I thoroughly brush my teeth, gargle with Lysol and tiptoe into the dark bedroom. My wife is already in bed. I can see in a beam of moonlight through the window that she is watching me. It is very important for me not to topple over while I undress or stagger when I traverse the few steps to the bed.

"Did you have a good time?" she asks coolly.

"I missed you," I say.

"I'll *bet*," says she as I slide in beneath the covers and snuggle up against her back and whisper to her something that I would very much like to do with her that we have never done before.

She looks over her shoulder with a smile of mild amusement. Clearly she feels the urgent sincerity of my desire. "Where did you ever get an idea like that?" she asks.

"I don't know," I say. "It just sort of occurred to me while I was walking home. It might be fun." I nuzzle her neck. "You know, honey, I have such a crush on you."

# Breakfast in Brighton

*Thomas McCarthy*

Somerset Maugham's advice to the visitor to England was succinct: "If you want to eat well have breakfast three times a day." And when I first came to live in England in the 1960s, the English breakfast was a fine meal. You began with a choice of porridge, stewed prunes, fresh grapefruit, followed by bacon, sausages, eggs, kidneys, mushrooms, tomatoes. Alternatively, you could choose from kippers, kedgeree, or smoked haddock with poached eggs, boiled or scrambled eggs, served with thick hot toast, fresh butter and Cooper's Oxford marmalade. Nowadays, the offerings in hotels, supermarket cafes and the "greasy spoon" cafes are dire —greasy bacon, eggs fried in a machine that either under or over cooks them, sawdust sausages, baked beans; scrambled eggs that are dry, rubbery and tasteless and soggy toast. A request for a boiled or poached egg is met with incomprehension. So when I received a request to write about my worst meal my initial response was, "Where the hell do I start?"

This decline in the availability of good food has been marked by a loss of traditional English dishes. Though many people, the French for one, regard English cooking as an insult to the stomach and palate, there are some excellent specialties. Scotch salmon, potted shrimps, braised oxtail, jugged hare, rack of Welsh lamb and roast chicken with bread sauce. Old favourites like Dover sole, steak, kidney and oyster pudding, and to finish, stilton cheese, treacle tart, or bread and butter pudding and the delectable summer pudding.

Although it is possible to find these dishes, most of them are usually available only in long-established and expensive restaurants, clubs and the old hotels mainly in London. In their place, there is a surfeit of ethnic food. If we decide to eat out locally and want to be sure of good food, we head for our favourite Indian, Chinese or Thai restaurant. Their owners are hands on, they cook or serve and are always in the restaurant; the quality of the food and service is high and consistent. To venture elsewhere is to take a risk. More than a risk if you are ignorant about the pub or restaurant. My rule of thumb when eating out in England is that if I find a good restaurant, I'm lucky, whereas on the continent if I have a bad meal, I'm unlucky.

The general indifference and ignorance about food by a majority of people is sometimes linked with the Industrial Revolution, when women worked long hours in factories, away from their homes and relied on cheap food to feed their families; and the dearth of affordable restaurants until about thirty years ago, when the first Chinese and Indian restaurants appeared. The confusion is apparent in the names of meals. The midday meal is lunch to some and dinner to others; in the evening, you may have dinner, tea or supper, according to local custom, unless you live in the north of England, where supper is a snack before bed. And there is the paradox that beside this poor food, there is the popularity of cookery shows on TV and massive sales of cookery books by celebrity chefs. Yet on a daily basis, people shovel in whatever is quick, filling and cheap, often from the plethora of fast food takeaways—Indian, Chinese, pizza, the ubiquitous McDonalds and greasy kebab shops popular after a night out. Even the fish-and-chip shop, once a working class source of cheap nutritional food, is more often than not a greasy foul dive. The queues for the traditional Friday evening meal of fish and chips wait in the streets seemingly oblivious to the stench of stale oil wafting overhead.

Pubs advertise two-course Sunday lunches at five pounds per head. Industrial catering suppliers often provide these meals; the only cooking necessary is the requisite time in a microwave, despite claims to be Home Cooked. An electrician doing some work in the house told me he had installed six industrial-size microwaves in a small local pub that advertises home cooking.

The abundance of cheap fatty food and a general ignorance of nutrition are noticeable in the increase in obesity, so acute the government has set up a public health campaign to encourage healthy eating.

The best food in England is in people's homes where the cook is a lover of good food. Today Maugham's advice to visitors would surely be: "If you want to eat well in England stay with a friend who enjoys cooking."

As I went back over the many dreadful meals I've endured when travelling on business or being entertained, I settled on three.

Dinner in the beautiful picturesque Welsh town of Betws-y-coed in Snowdonia after a day's hiking. Sole Veronique, which I had not seen on a menu for years, was not fillets of sole poached in a wine and fish bouillon but a whole plaice fried in batter and served submerged in a watery grey sauce in which nestled four grapes cut in half. A wedding in a beautiful old country house hotel, where the main course of roast beef and Yorkshire pudding, one of the glories of English food, was overcooked slices of cheap stewing beef coated in viscous gravy.

And there was breakfast in Brighton.

Some years ago, I went to read at the Brighton Literary Festival and my hosts arranged and paid for my overnight accommodation in a B&B. After I checked in to my small room at the rear of the house with views of slate roofs and seagulls, the landlady demanded what time I wanted breakfast. With a late night ahead, I suggested 9 o'clock.

"My other guest," she sniffed, "is having his at 7.30."

"Okay, 7.30 then," I said, anxious to get away.

My bed, when I got to it after midnight, was hard, the blankets thin; there was no hot water then or in the morning. I stubbed a toe on a chair and banged my head on a beam on my bleary way to breakfast the next morning. I was not, in my father's phrase after a heavy night, "in the fullness of my health."

At 7.30, the dining room was deserted; a solitary place was set for breakfast. After a moment, the landlady came in and said, "Help yourself to orange juice and cereal."

When I had briefly spoken to her the previous evening I thought she reminded me of somebody I knew. Now I decided she resembled Olga from Russia, as we called the fierce matron of the hospital where an uncle of mine referred his patients and with whom he threatened my brother and I when we misbehaved. The realisation that there might be more than one Olga made my hangover suddenly a lot worse.

The juice, in a minuscule glass, tasted of cheap watered squash. I skipped the supermarket cornflakes in the battered packet standing by a single bowl and waited as Olga returned with a rack of toast and a pot of coffee. I poured some coffee, took a sip and said, "This is tea."

"You ordered tea," Olga snapped.

"I never drink tea, I don't like it."

She snatched the pot and returned in a few minutes with the same pot and with my breakfast on a plate which she held in a tea towel.

A strip of streaky bacon barely cooked, an unappetising pink sausage, raw in places, an egg fried so hard I suspected it was reheated from the previous day, a spoonful of tinned tomatoes whose juice left a rusty scar across the plate and a slice of fried bread with the consistency of concrete. The plate was so hot the juice from the tomatoes bubbled faintly. My appetite vanished but not my hunger; I drank some coffee, tepid, cheap instant powder tasting strongly of tea.

There were bottles of tomato ketchup and brown sauce on the table. I poured a generous dollop over the breakfast and when the mess on the plate was covered, it did appear somewhat appetising. Then I surreptitiously looked around the room. There was an old dresser, dusty and uncared for in the corner. Carefully I opened the middle drawer and slid the food off the plate into it.

When Olga returned she looked at my empty plate with a mixture of surprise and suspicion. "Finished? Everything all right?"

"Delicious," I said.

# There but for the Grace:
## First Thanksiving

### *Mimi Schwartz*

I'd mastered macaroni and cheese, scrambled eggs, and hamburgers, but sixteen months into marriage, the haute cuisine of Thanksgiving was not in my repertoire. Not even memories of it. My mother must have made turkey with accessories every November, but all my food memories conjure up *Sauerbraten, Kartoffelsalat* and *Linzertorte*, not a slow-roasting bird in the oven. Ours, as you can tell, was a German cuisine, my parents having come to America in 1937, thee years before I was born.

I do remember eating sweet potatoes with marshmallows, but that was served as leftovers at my friend Arlene's house. Delicious. Which is why I included it on my first Thanksgiving menu, using a recipe from my neighbor Debbie who also gave me her secret for 'homemade' cranberry sauce from a can.

Debbie grew up in Iowa cooking everything, while I, in Queens, New York, only knew how to dry dishes—and occasionally help my mother make *Laugenbrezels*, big wads of dough we rolled, curled and baked into golden brown pretzels. That was fun, but everything else in the kitchen I thought dull for the American cowgirl I was meant to be. I charged with the boys through vacant lots, like the Lone Ranger, facing daily tests of bravery and high moral courage, while my mother, the cook, stayed in her kitchen, safe and untested.

Or so I thought until the day my husband Stu invited his graduate school professor and his wife over for Thanksgiving dinner.

We had decided not to take the thirteen-hour drive from Ann Arbor, Michigan to New York to eat with our parents, and Professor R and his wife were going to be alone, so Stu asked them, just like that. "She's bringing the pumpkin pie," he soothed, as I dumped unpacked wedding boxes, looking for cookbooks.

But by two p.m. on Thanksgiving Day, I was cautiously optimistic. With tips from the butcher (rub butter inside and out), twenty calls to my mother, and Debbie next door, I had the stuffed turkey roasting in the oven, a Jello/nut mold (my mother-in-law's recipe) thickening in the refrigerator, and cranberry-orange sauce beside it, made the day before after I had stuffed the turkey. I was folding mini marshmallows into sweet potatoes, humming along with the radio, when a news flash interrupted Frank Sinatra or someone equally calming about love. A bad lot of canned cranberries were proving toxic, the announcer warned grimly, and people—I think he mentioned Texas—had been hospitalized. Everyone was to check the serial numbers on the cans.

My two cranberry cans were in the middle of student housing's garbage dumpster, so I immediately thought—and so easily—*Why take a chance?* I'd read that the Pilgrims on their first Thanksgiving might have poisoned the Wampanoag chiefs on purpose, and I wasn't about to do the same. (So much for all those Thanksgiving plays about Indians and Pilgrims being kind together!) No, we would buy safe cans of cranberries if Krogers Supermarket was still open, and if not we would manage without, especially since the Jello was also red. We didn't need two dishes the same color.

My moral compass was steady as I set the dinette table, hoping the paper turkey I bought as a centerpiece didn't take up too much room. The real turkey was browning nicely, and so I went next door to warn Debbie about the cranberries. I could have told her through the paper-thin walls (this was Quonset-hut housing leftover from World War II), but I was ready for a coffee break. Three hours to go, and all I had left to do was to watch the turkey, remake the cranberry sauce, and open the Del Monte green beans. No one had warned against those cans.

"Are you all set?" Debbie asked. She had finished her chestnut soufflé and was chopping orange peel to add to the cranberries. That was her secret ingredient, shared with me.

"I am...was—until I heard the news broadcast. Did you know that people are being poisoned by canned cranberries?"

"You're fine. Don't sweat it." Debbie had already called Krogers, and their cans came from a different lot. They told her the bad numbers and she checked them against her cans.

"I can't check mine. For once, I was organized-- and made my sauce yesterday."

"Not to worry." She started to pour us coffee. "It's people stuffing their turkey early, sometimes two or three days before they roast it, that's the real killer."

"Why is that?" I asked, trying for innocence. I was glad that I'd only admitted to one-day-old cranberry sauce, nothing more.

"Raw eggs and bread sitting together inside a turkey is a no no. *That* can really cause botulism. And salmonella. Bad stuff." She pushed the cookie jar towards me: "My aunt had a neighbor who pre-stuffed a turkey and all her...." *My sweet, stuffed, 15 pound turkey, poison?* I stood up, refusing to believe it, and backed towards the door. "I forgot. I have to baste my turkey! Happy Thanksgiving!" I said. And I was out of there.

Debbie *was being overly cautious. That was probably an Iowa kitchen tale.* I dialed my mother to affirm this, but hung up on the first ring. I dialed Stu in his campus office, so he could pick up safe cranberry cans on his way home *Should he pick up two pizzas just in case?*—and hung up again. I pictured throwing my turkey in the dumpster in back and couldn't do it. It looked so perfect.

I removed the paper turkey centerpiece and put down the Jello mold that had stayed together when I flipped it. My mother-in-law said that hers once slipped into the sink and halfway down the drain before she salvaged enough to serve in individual bowls. Mine had landed perfectly. The cranberry sauce, beside it, looked lusciously healthy. (Krogers had closed early, so I decided to trust Debbie about the safety of my cranberry cans.) Stu was carving the beautiful turkey while I got the sweet potato casserole, still bubbling. "Oh, it looks delicious! Everything smells wonderful!" I heard as I solemnly served the stuffing.

*Botulism only happens after two or three days inside the raw turkey, Debbie said. My stuffing was in there less than one day. It must be fine*! I told myself after I came from home from Debbie's, opened the oven door, and saw my turkey skin, so crisp and shiny. *It must be fine*, I whispered now over the cranberry sauce. And as I scooped the golden stuffing onto every plate. And as I watched Stu swallow the first bite of drumstick, his favorite. And as Prof R drowned his breast meat in cranberry sauce.

When Mrs. R., tasting the stuffing, wanted the recipe, I said, "Oh, it's on the Wonder Bread bag," and forcing a smile, I switched to *Whatever will be, we will live or die together*. I lifted my fork, ready to stab the white meat on my plate, but it stayed in mid-air. I lowered it, but it landed on the green beans. A minute later I tried again, aiming for the stuffing; but it speared the sweet potatoes. Everyone's plate was emptying, but mine, aside from two bare spots, stayed full. I couldn't eat more—even as I pictured myself as a widow, in jail.

All night I watched my husband to be sure he was breathing, and the next morning I called Prof. and Mrs. R. All had survived except my heroic sense of self, which, like the Lone Ranger of my childhood, had disappeared for good. In its stead was a spineless wimp of twenty-two, who not only avoided the risky stuffed turkey, but the almost safe cranberry sauce! Inexcusable. And worse, early the next morning with Stu still in bed, I threw Thanksgiving into the dumpster, prepared to say that the refrigerator door had been open all night and everything spoiled. I don't think I was getting rid of the evidence, but anything was possible with the new gastronomical me.

Since then my stuffing bakes alone, and I try to have a back-up like Indonesian chicken thighs, frozen. So it is safe to come to my house for dinner. But I wouldn't blame you if you didn't eat what I didn't eat. Isn't that what the Indian chiefs and the Roman emperors figured out, although mostly too late?

# Bang, Boot, Man, Woman

*Steve Davenport*

Bang, bang go the boots on the wooden floor of the Courier Café twenty-five years ago.

Call them what you will. Man Boots. Macho Boots. Boots of the Booted Husband.

Booted as in rejected or ejected from the marital bed. Booted as in kicked to the curb.

But booted also in that I'm wearing those boots and they're making a rough song as I walk, one bang after another across that wooden floor, the sound up in my head like fists in a drum. Not a working man's shit-kickers, but Timberlands, wheat-colored, marker of grad-school hipness circa 1985. Bang and bang go the boots and the floor of the Courier Café in Urbana, Illinois, as I approach the table and my last chance. I mean I'm carrying a load of timber that long afternoon from the Land of Marital Separation to the Table of Two Women. Timber as in the trees, the material, the history I've cleared, the emotional debris post-tornado, just to walk into that restaurant for a lunch that might result—might, I say, might—in a triangulated relationship that solves and saves everything. Most things anyway. Timber as in the stuff we use to make new stuff, in this case a new marital arrangement out of a failed old, but timber also as in wood, as in the full extension of fleshy possibility. My own.

I'm talking manly tumescence. Ripe and growing full for the opportunity.

Bang goes my heart as I arrive at the table, where the two

women sit with menus before them. To my right is my wife of four years, a woman with whom I haven't lived for months. To my left is the other woman. Or another woman. But not just any woman. This woman's Bisexual Woman. She's the friend my wife sent to my apartment door a few weeks back to say hi, to introduce herself, to fill a space I'm thinking my wife imagined empty, and surely, though this part went unspoken, to fuck me. If not that night, soon. A nod to guilt, an act of control, an apology maybe, but a gift also from an old friend.

The woman who knocked on my door that evening was, at first glance, a pizza boy at the wrong address. Except the boy was carrying no pizza. Except the boy spoke my first name in an overly familiar way. Except the boy's voice was oddly deep and not a boy's at all. It was an adult voice. Before me, there in the hall of my apartment building, where I thought I saw pizza, a sexy enough vision given the few dollars I had left after I made rent on the apartment I was now solely responsible for, there across the threshold, not three feet away, was a woman. In the hall. Having just knocked on my door and looking for me. On a Saturday night. How pathetic that she knew I'd be there alone, but still, a woman knocking.

It was only the third time anyone had knocked on my door since my wife had moved across town. Each time it was a woman. The second time was actually two women. Assuming the knock was my wife's, hopefully, stupidly assuming, I hurried out of the shower. Maybe something had changed. Maybe she'd collected some magic words that would put Humpty Dumpty back together again. Even when I glimpsed two bodies through the keyhole, women's bodies, neither of them my wife's, and knew my assumption to be another sad wish, I didn't wait for the information to process. I flipped the lock and pulled on the knob like some people step in front of a car that appears out of nowhere not because it's a good idea but because they've already begun the motion and stopping it awkwardly would not be cool. I opened the door in a towel. One of the women was black, the other white. Both wore white blouses, one a skirt, the other businesslike slacks, and both women were as pretty as I was dripping wet. They were also Jehovah Witnesses who left politely but sooner than they might have. They did not ask if they could come in. I might have offered, but I figured The Lord was going to win that round.

The first person to knock on my door, maybe two months into our separation, was my wife. When I answered, a fearful face turned angry. She saw immediately that I was alive. She told me with heat that my mother and a sister had been unable to get me on the phone for some time and wanted her to see if I was all right (code for alive, code for not a suicide). Apparently my mother and sister wanted confirmation before they troubled themselves with a 160-mile drive. You know, to go all that way and be disappointed. It turns out I'd knocked the phone off the hook in the master bedroom a couple of weeks before and hadn't noticed that no one was calling to see if I was dead. What I couldn't say is that I'd abandoned the big bedroom for a four-person tent I'd bought on sale and set up in the second bedroom. I apologized for the phone because I didn't know what else to say, and she left.

This third time, the woman at the door, the woman who was not a pizza boy, was either, I figured, my wife's lover or an ex-lover. Or maybe a would-be lover, though "lover" didn't seem to be the right word for it. In fact, "lover" was and is a silly word for what I'm talking about. The two women at the Courier Café table may or may not have had sex. As I'm walking across the floor, I'm pretty sure that if anything physical had happened between them it was over. I'm pretty sure the second woman, Bisexual Woman, wanted something more from my wife, some emotional webbing to invite and pull together physical moments, make of them a structure capable of sustaining a relationship, a strong, spidery crossbeam in their own House of Love. But I'm thinking, or maybe I've been told by my wife, that they, the two women, have no webbing that binds

83

them, that my wife isn't interested in Bisexual Woman.

Then why are we all here? What could possibly come of such a meeting? Why are my boots so loud and why does the Bang, Bang sound like Man, Man? Why do I suddenly not want to be there? Though my wife and I had been powerfully close early on and for many of our friends and family the two halves that fit perfectly together with the wet, clicking noise that accompanies that sort of thing, we were never matched in bed. Not before I gave her that Adrienne Rich calendar for Christmas and read aloud "Diving into the Wreck," the Rich poem I wish I'd written. And certainly not during the next few months in which everything fell apart and she fell out of the closet she didn't even know she was sitting in.

Why do I suddenly not want to be there? Why did I ever want to be there? Bisexual Woman and I have a friendship my wife may or may not know about. The details. The hanging out and the sex. What happens if my wife doesn't know and would be bothered if she did? What if she asks me point-blank there at the table in front of Bisexual Woman, who may or may not want her to know? Maybe they've talked about it and it's no big deal until I lie when asked. Why don't I plan better? Why am I the last to arrive if I'm five minutes early? Why does the table of two women look like a trap? Maybe I've set the trap. Maybe I'm the spider and they're the bait I'm using to catch me. Or maybe the table's not so much a trap as it is a really, really bad idea. Am I a coward? Is that why I want to leave? And why not leave, just turn and walk away?

Because I'm already in motion in that direction, toward the table, and I don't know how to make the turning around mean something I could articulate if asked. I don't know how to make it look meaningful. Not to mention cool.

And what, by the way, am I to do with a menu? Can I afford anything on it? If I can, will what I eat mark me as a man, as in the Other? Bang, Bang, Man, Man.

I make two key mistakes when I sit down and they both involve

84

the waitress. Within a minute of my nodding hi and looking down at a menu, the waitress walks up behind me or to the side of me, just out of my line of vision, and says, "Are you ready to order?" Without thinking or rather thinking that she's asking me specifically since, after all, my early arrival has made me I don't know how many minutes late, I say, "No." Then I hear my wife through the thick, frosty air enveloping our table, "You're speaking for everyone?" If things get any thicker, colder, denser, more difficult to see and move through, I'm going to reach into my man boots, the right one since I'm right-handed, and find the machete every man, every man's man, keeps there for those moments when only a machete will do. I will use it to cut the ties that bind us, to whack through the icy overgrowth, to make the table a more hospitable place for three people to negotiate over lunch a triangulated solution to an old problem. I will save the day.

Except I have no machete. Except I'm not sitting on a hero's silver stallion and if anyone needs saving it's me. Except when the waitress takes the orders of the two women and turns to me, I say, "Nothing. Just water." I have made my second mistake. I have refused to break bread with them. What I do then is speak the truth. I say I have almost no money. The money I have goes to the rent I can't afford and that four-person tent I bought to go with the machete-less hiking boots that are really loud. I say I knew I wouldn't be able to afford lunch here, so I ate a can of chili before I left the apartment. Chili Man, I say. My favorite. I always say "Chili Man" because I like Chili Man and want everyone else to like it too.

No one says anything. Except when my wife does. She says, "You mean you came here to meet us for lunch and now you refuse to eat lunch with us?" I sit there wondering about lunch and what it means exactly, its social purpose, how it sets up expectations and obligations and, on occasion, opportunities. I think of all the timber I cleared, the emotional work I did to make it through the last few months and walk into the restaurant for a last chance at what? I have no idea. Happiness? I don't know what form that happiness would take, but I realize while I'm looking at the glass of water I now don't want to touch, I should have stayed with Chili Man. I should be eating Chili Man right now in my tent. Not out of a can. I'm no savage.

Bang, Bang, Man, Man.

# Her Very Worst Meal and How It Was Much Like the Three Fat Men—One of Whom Was Wearing a Beret—She Saw Today

*Renée Ashley*

> *A daydream is a meal at which images are eaten.*
> —W. H. Auden

She eats for comfort. She eats for camaraderie. She eats out of boredom, habit, convenience, and, even occasionally, hunger. She eats to procrastinate. She eats too much. She eats too fast. There's very little she chooses not to eat—though on that one hand, blackeyed peas are a major unfavorite (that's a first-husband story, but she would never have liked them anyway). Lemon grass, all things perfumy-tasting she finds unpleasant. Gin. Though she could choke it all down if the need arose. Who knows ... they might taste better than they did before. They might be fine. And fine is just fine. She doesn't need fancy or expensive, she doesn't need great. She just needs to get through the day.

And on the other hand, there are foods she is drawn to. Grapefruit. Spicy red beans with or without rice. Fresh purple figs.

White bean soup. And cake. Chicken chili. Mangoes. And bread. Pepper Jack cheese. And cheddar. Hamburgers. Turkey sandwiches. Horseradish sauce on rare roast beef. Or Tabasco. Manwich Sloppy Joes. She's had roasted lamb and thought it was delicious until she pictured the lamb. Frozen pot pies, chicken best. Corn dogs! Beets. Potstickers. Ramen noodles. Sweet and sour. She's allergic to peanuts and that's a damn shame because peanut butter is love. Tacos! She adores tuna casserole concocted with frozen peas and canned cream of mushroom soup (especially if the egg noodles are the really wide ones) topped with potato chips which are smooshed and crunchy. Apricots. Liverwurst. Lima beans cooked in plain tap water just with chopped onion (dehydrated is fine) and maybe, but not necessarily, a hambone. Fish fingers. TV dinners (Salisbury steak or fried chicken best, Banquet brand, the cheap ones: a staple of her childhood). She's not fussy, not particular. You can't say she's indiscriminate, however—because she doesn't really want to face those blackeyed peas.

Perhaps you could call her *open-endedly-barely-discriminate* or maybe *generous-in-her-tastes-despite-biases-but-also-taking-into-consideration-the-circumstances.* In all likelihood, she'll eat it, whatever it is, even if she bitches about it during or afterwards. She's a good-time eater and a bad-time eater—her mother's response to any tension (there was always tension) was "Have a sandwich," and she did. She doesn't send food back. She chews and she swallows and she does it again.

The upshot? Food, for her, is mostly forgettable. One obvious exception might be the sashimi she could barely choke down when a kind college professor, a generous woman who was trying to widen the unworldly girl's experience, took her out to lunch. The professor did the ordering; the girl's stomach rose and threatened to spill with every bite. But she bit. And she kept it down. To not do so would have been unforgivable.

But on just about any day, Wendy's is or would be great. Never a problem: just give her some Asian-Style Boneless Chicken Wings and a chocolate Frosty. Or the quotidian paradox: the Diet Coke Frosty float. She'll be happy. A Burger King burger and a medium Diet Coke runs a close second.

She considers herself an *easy* eater. And she thinks her friends do too. But easy isn't how one man in particular, sees it. He has been stricken by the vast spectrum of her unfussiness for years. And so, through him, she was made aware of the *what-was-exceptional*: her most notable meal, her absolute worst plate of food ever.

Which she simply chose not to eat.

And she thought nothing of that decision until the above-unnamed man, after having already distanced himself from his plate with a moan of dismay so loud, and a strangled look of such complete revulsion, that the whole table he sat at in the refectory—maybe twenty adults?—turned their attention down the long board towards him. At that moment, she had just been sitting down at the table next to the crucible of their curiosity. She was about to dig in.

And she still has trouble understanding how that mild meal of leftovers could have been as revolting as it genuinely was. When she thinks of it, she thinks of it euphemistically as *Stuff in Sauce*—a mélange of leftover breakfast meats along with some potato. But not hash. She *likes* hash. This was a kind of maudlin stew of leftovers. And she knows leftovers to be a proud tribe and worthy—and these appeared to be perfectly fine leftovers until they were *glacéd*, it seemed, in some sort of gray, translucent medium, something that resembled a reduction of dirty bucket water. It was viscous, shiny, and the only taste it had was somewhere between dust and phlegm, something she could only at the time call *Oh-Christ-No-I-Can't-Eat-That*. The shining misery of the gravy had penetrated the meat scraps and clung—some mysterious, probably chemical (and perhaps dangerous) adhesion had taken place. She'd tried scraping it off, but each pass left only a slightly thinner, somewhat more roughened-up and ghastly-looking sheath of bucket-gray slime on the meat. There wasn't a chance in hell of saving a piece of over-cooked potato.

She worked diligently at the larger bits of meat, though, and with good faith, but finally had to concede defeat: the dish was clearly a product of some bad wizard and, as she watched it congeal, she was certain it developed a supernatural aura of smugness.

After she had finally sighed and settled her flatware on her plate, leveraged it out a bit towards the center of the table, and reached for her cup of black tea, she realized her seatmate had been studying her intently as she'd tried to salvage her bacon. Then he said to the air that hung over the table in front of them both: "Even she won't eat it—well, that proves it."

She was taken aback only a bit. She wasn't sure what it proved, but she wasn't willing to eat what was on her plate just to disprove it.

Something in her, though, had been jostled at the recognition that a dish prepared to be eaten could be so utterly inedible. An anomaly had, without any effort on her part, lifted itself from her slough of blind habit and presented itself in an uncustomary glow. A little bit like an insight. She gave a small mental gasp, but had no idea what she should do with the information.

So today she was driving to the market—it was either throw something quick together for dinner or pick up a pizza again, she hadn't yet decided—when she saw the backs of three fat men walking at the side of the non-residential, no-sidewalk, low-rent exurban road, and she had a feeling of déjà vu. All three of the men wore what appeared to be identical light gray business suits. The fabric seemed a little shiny but it may have just been the sun. The middle man, an inch or two shorter than the others, was wearing a black beret. She could tell from the backs of their heads, all three were balding. They wore black shoes, their cuffs swept their dusty heels, and they walked in extremely close proximity to one another, as though they had their arms around one another's waists. She felt it again, that sensation she'd had at the refectory table: a recognition rising above her vast daily midden of preoccupation and mindlessness. It was as though a proverbial fog had suddenly lifted.

Those men did not belong; they were aliens in any way one might choose to define the word, or they had slipped, perhaps, from an alternate version of Lewis Carroll (Tweedle Dum, Tweedle Dee, and ...Tweedle Three?), or, more realistically, they were out-of-town (or out-of-work) real estate men—from an office with an unfortunate dress code—assessing the dried-mud, acre-plus lot in front of the low, cinder block building that housed the defunct mechanic's shop and the hut behind which had served for not too long as a dog-grooming parlor. The point being: they stood out. They were what made that day different. They were anomalous and snagged her attention. *They made her look. They made her think.*

She was late getting to the market. She'd forgotten what she'd gone there for. She bought a Diet Coke in a small, plastic bottle, drank it in the car in the parking lot while she watched the seagulls circle the Chinese restaurant, and went home. She ate hummus and ginger snaps for dinner. She still sees the men in her mind.

Imagine, then, the upshots of such recognition: contingency and its seatmate opportunity arranged around thought like this: anomaly and image, and the banquet of possibilities thereof—a quote from Auden's *The Dyer's Hand,* some appalling gravy, and three fat men—one of whom was wearing a beret—who just did not belong.

# Hell Broth and Poisoned Entrails:
## An Affair with Scottish Cookery

*Susan Tekulve*

During the first week of April 2009, my husband, son and I lived in a flat in Old Town Edinburgh, on the Royal Mile, across from the World's End Close, an alley named so because it was once the very edge of the original town, and therefore the very edge of the world to the town's original inhabitants. Along a street lined with whiskey shops, and up three flights of stairs, we found our flat called "The Story Teller's Apartment." The apartment was freshly painted white, its bedroom filled with a high, soft bed and a window seat overlooking a bright blue pub called "The World's End." Our landlady, Fiona, had left us a hand-typed list of sites and amenities called "Fiona's Favorites," which read, "There's a wee shop on the corner where you can buy groceries. If it's whiskey you're after, I'd suggest the Royal Mile Whiskies."

My husband, Rick, was unpacking his suitcase, folding sweaters into a pine chest in the bedroom. I knew he was plotting a trip to those whiskey shops. I had only a dim notion of what I was after. As Edinburgh's native son, the writer Robert Louis Stevenson, once wrote, "The great affair of travel is to move; to feel the needs and hitches of our own life more nearly; to come down off this feather-bed of civilization, and find the globe granite underfoot and strewn with cutting stone." I skimmed down "Fiona's Favorites" until I found a listing for "The Real Mary King's Close: An Historically

Accurate Interpretation of 16th through 19th century Edinburgh. Witness the highs and lows of sixteenth-century town houses. Visit the home of a grave digger's family to discover the truth about how the Burgh council dealt with the plague of 1645." I reread the words "plague" and "grave digger," knowing only that I wanted to move deeper into the cold, cut stone of one of Europe's most storied cities.

"This looks really good," I said. "You want to go here first?"

"I've always wanted to see that," my husband said.

We walked up the street to "The Real Mary King's Close"and booked a tour for the next morning. While in the gift shop, we picked up a free membership to The Friends of the Classic Malts Club, receiving a flavor map of Scottish whiskeys. My husband prefers the island malts, the heavily-peated ones hinting of ocean brine. He likes feeling as if he's swallowing a bonfire while sipping whiskey, tasting the ashes of an ancient hearth at the back of his throat. Though not a whiskey drinker, I enjoy watching Rick take pleasure in his favorite drink, this Scottish "water of life." I followed him gamely in and out of the whiskey shops along the Royal Mile, making friends with the shopkeepers who poured generous samples of any whiskey we wanted into drams, saying, "Give this one a nose. Then take a wee taste and let it warm the back of your throat."

Around the fourth shop, I discovered a whiskey I actually liked, a lower highland malt called Auchentoshan. The color of honey, it tasted of heather and pears. Its heat was as mellow as evening sunlight. Warmed by my newfound fondness for lowland whiskey, my husband proudly bought me my own ladylike bottle of twelve-year-old Auchentoshan, 750 milliters to take back to the Story Teller's Apartment and drink.

All our fifteen-year-old son wanted to do that day was eat. Fearless as his name, Hunter would eat haggis for breakfast, lunch and dinner if we had regular access to it, never mind that this dish is made from a sheep's heart, liver and lungs minced together, mixed with onion and oatmeal, stuffed into the sheep's plucked stomach.

After whiskey shopping, we took Hunter down to the farmers market behind Edinburgh Castle and bought him a bag of Scotch eggs—boiled eggs dipped in beaten egg, rolled in mace-seasoned sausage, dipped again in more beaten egg, then deep fried. We bought a black-faced sheep and mustard pie, links of blood sausage, homemade short bread.

On our way back to the Story Teller's Apartment, we stopped at a cheesemonger's shop for a wedge of Lanark Blue Cheese, mould-ripened and made from unpasteurised ewes' milk.

None of these traditional foods taste bad; my difficulty with Scottish cookery is that these dishes were developed for heartier appetites of roving clan members, the strong stomachs of farm hands who cooked lamb and grains together in iron pots over open fires after a day spent harvesting five hundred bales of hay. An Italian American accustomed to fish, pasta and olive oil, I usually sip the Scotch broth and head straight for the safety of shortbread when in Scotland. That evening, my twelve-year-old lowland whisky opened up with a drop of water and revealed the pleasures of minced organ meats, making everything go down quite easily. Sipping whiskey from a coffee cup, I ate the unpasteurized cheese, a Scotch egg, a slice of sheep pie, the haggis and cullen skink, ( fish, potato and onion soup). Savoring a finger of shortbread with one last cup of whiskey, I had a revelation: Collops in a pan were really just a variation of the Italian peasant dish, osso bucco. A clootie dumpling was quite similar to an Italian panna cotta. Eating while under the influence of lowland whiskey, I had a revelation: Scottish cooking, inspired by French cooking, must have been born of Italian chefs 200 years ago!

I fell asleep early that night, but I awoke sweating at 10 p.m., throat burning from flames that must have lain dormant beneath that sweet lowland whiskey. My head and heart pounded to the sound of late-night patrons stumbling out of the World's End Pub across the street. I'd slept hard, with my left arm bent oddly beneath me, and it was hanging numb and heavy at my side. Not wanting to wake Rick or Hunter, I decided to sit on the window seat and read myself back to sleep by the glow of the street lamp. I pulled down one of the books from Fiona's bookshelf, *The Town Below the Ground*, and opened it to a chapter about the plague victims of Mary King's Close. According to this book, the plague of 1645 spread quickly by fleas that fed off infected rats. The inhabitants of Mary King's Close who suffered from the plague were sealed inside their own houses, a red cross and the words "God have Mercy" painted across their doors. Two months later, when the city council felt it safe to remove the bodies, rigor mortis had taken hold. Death cart labourers dismembered the corpses with axes and hauled the remains away in any kind of improvised shroud.

I shut the book, feeling strange hitches in my body, my abdomen cinched too tightly to my esophagus, my heart, liver and lungs surely poisoned by the diseased organs of the countless Scottish farm animals I'd eaten a few hours before. A needling fire had risen up my deadened left arm, stiffening my neck, fevering my pounding head. I ran to the bathroom and looked in the mirror, saw what looked like a plague victim -- blotchy skin, witchy hair, tiny broken blood vessels in eyes gritty in their sockets. I went back to the window seat, opened *The Town Below the Ground* and read about Bubonic plague symptoms: fever, head and muscle ache, abdominal pain, thirst, delirium, a stiff neck and an intense desire to sleep, which, if yielded to, quickly proved fatal. I read about the infamous buboes, tender nodes growing in the underarms and necks of the plague victims, ranging from one to ten centimeters in size. I did not have any buboes. I lay back on the soft tartan bed, dizzily relieved. God have Mercy, I thought. Slowly, slowly, near dawn, I yielded to sleep.

The next morning, I awoke free of muscle ache and fever, but shaky and swollen, my stomach as changeable as Scottish spring weather. During the ten-minute walk to Mary King's Close, we witnessed white mist, chill drizzle, clouds threading and scudding across a round, brilliant sun holding itself just above the pointiest spire of Saint Giles Cathedral. These inclement feelings lingered within me at the tour entrance. We were greeted by a college kid dressed up in period costume, playing a plague cleaner who took us down into his home, a low tenement house he shared with 12 other people. He explained how he bathed in fish oil and emptied his chamber pot into an alley that flowed to the Nor Loch, the body of water outside the Flodden Wall that surrounded the original city. He said that the plague of 1645 was caused by cramp and filth inside the Flodden Wall, and that the rampant disease whittled 40,000 citizens down to 60, solving the city's problems with overcrowding.

The tour ended in a bed chamber filled with wax dummies suffering from various stages of plague. A silent figure wearing a long dark robe with a pointed hood, leather gloves and a beak-shaped mask walked into the room. Our guide introduced him as Dr. George Ray, the famous plague doctor. As the hooded figure ministered to the wax plague victims, draining the buboes around their necks, our guide said that the doctor had filled his beak mask with broom, an herb thought to protect against the plague. The doctor didn't know the disease was carried by infected fleas; his sinister wardrobe simply guarded him against the fleas, the herbs merely masking the smell of the black ooze coming from the victims as he lanced and bled them. The guide "debunked" the popular story that the city council sealed up any plague area, sentencing its victims and their families to die inside.

"This is myth," he said, almost proudly, explaining that the victims were only quarantined in their own homes with their families. They simply had to wave a white flag outside their open window and lower a basket to someone on the street who would fill it with bread and water, sometimes a little wine. IF a victim survived, she received a certificate of health and resumed a normal life.

Though mercifully short, the underground plague tour had left me feeling cold and sleepy. As we walked out into the street, I found myself voicing a callous thought: "Well, I guess if you've seen one plague victim you've seen them all. Where to next?"

Hunter voted to go eat more haggis; Rick wanted to check out a few more whiskey shops. The smell of haggis wafted from an open pub door, making my throat and stomach twitch in a bad, familiar way. I considered fleeing back to The Story Teller's Apartment, quarantining myself and waving a white flag, lowering a basket out the window, down to the street for Rick and Hunter to fill with bread and water as they passed by on their way for more haggis and whiskey. But we were moving away from the Royal Mile, along a crooked street toward a crowd gathered on the sidewalk before a shop. The crowd was admiring a one hundred pound roasted pig displayed in the window, a sweet-faced shop girl who smiled and plucked side meat from the pig, mounding it on a bun, topping it all off with a slice of thick, roasted pig skin. The shop was called "Oink," and its sign boasted the house specialty, a "Delicious Crackling Hog Roast Roll." As Rick and Hunter moved through the shop door, I stepped away from the pig, assessing my limitations. I felt as if I'd been granted a certificate of health that day; it was beginning to seem possible to resume a normal life. I could not eat a crackling hog roll.

Instead, I offered to go back to the Royal Mile and book a day trip to Pitlochery, the gateway to the Highlands, a short tour that would take us through Birnum Wood, where Shakespeare set MacBeth. Double, double, toil and trouble, I thought. After a night of hell broth and poisoned entrails, a morning of underground filth and spectacle, I wanted only outside air, earth beneath my feet, elevation. An ancient disease requires an ancient cure--walking. After booking the tour, I walked past our apartment, beyond the World's End Close, down to the Southeast end of the Royal Mile to a park surrounding the base of a dormant volcano called Arthur's Seat. Plump, moody clouds scudded across the blue sky, and a soft breeze roused the yellow broom blazing from the volcano's lower cliffs, infusing the air with the scent of coconut. I plucked a few broom blossoms and put them in my pocket. For the rest of the trip, I carried the broom like talismans, fragrant guards against the highs and lows of Scottish cookery.

# A Flood of Doom

## Wallis Wilde-Menozzi

Asked about a worst meal, my first thought is that it depends on what worst means. I have only fasted twice, but no meal can be worse than having no food, or having unsafe water, and living with chronic weakness and the uncertainty of hunger. My life in Italy, where a worst meal is nearly impossible, has taught me deep respect for food and this focus is not the moralistic one linked to my childhood. Concern for the millions who are hungry has to do with inclusion, love, and sharing.

That said, hoping to have drawn a distinction, I ask myself again, worst in which sense? When I was held upside down over a lake and hit on the back because I had a fishbone in my throat? When the butcher sold my turkey and I had twenty people coming for dinner? I am still drawn to an early attitude of mine. It's an image of feet firmly planted and an ability to pack my cheeks and never swallow. It's a dark storm of silence and waiting in front of a bowl of cereal that to "nothingness did sink." In a family blessed with resources, I had rickets, was hospitalized for malnutrition, developed an ulcer, in spite of my steady climb to a height of nearly six feet. At the ages of two and three I used to watch my breakfast cereal collapse in its first five minutes of puffiness, and from then on, the gray little swamp it became was a moral issue that kept me staring into its thick shallowness, sometimes for up to eight hours. The cycle was not broken when I went to school. I missed whole days because I could not leave the table until I finished. So one worst meal is breakfast. Always. There was not the saving island of even a piece of toast.

Another angle would be cooking. There I find the radiant impulses of generosity and sharing that are intrinsic to food. I had not grown up with vegetables or many fruits. My mother rushed towards American progress and she bought a freezer of Icelandic size. We had TV dinners and never any guests. An ability to choose between chicken and beef prepared my brothers and me for the future world of frequent flyer miles. Innocents, we thought spaghetti was a variegated column, just as it slipped from a can, and cranberry, a marble cylinder. Potatoes came from a box as flakes to which you added water. So upon leaving home, I was thrilled and fascinated by the beauty and variety of the skins and colors of fruits and vegetables: the crevices in spinach, the fuzziness of a peach. Then there were endless new species altogether—eggplants, artichokes, garlic, grapes, basil, zucchini, cabbage, mushrooms, lamb, pears, plums, sole, scallops, yogurt, crusty bread. Not to mention, coffee, teas, and wines. I realize that the 1960s and 70s brought to many parts of the world a set of choices in ingredients that grew beyond the local, or the seasonal, as the western world began to grow richer. Sophistication reached the suburbs, too.

The first meal I offered stays as a sort of record. Lacking culture in food, without training, but with a warm heart that believed food is a way to reach people, I moved enthusiastically towards cooking, in some ways as if it were painting. I put colors together and textures. Unfortunately, since I was unschooled, my first meal remained one about inexperience, old habits and an interest in saving time. It was prepared for a young man whom I loved and to whom I offered leaks, potatoes and a fried egg. Those ingredients hardly seem inspiring, but for me a potato with its knobs and eyes, and a leek with its braided leaves, and a free range egg seemed quite miraculous in that they were real food and came from an open market. What was missing was how you prepare things, and the place that preparation plays. I rinsed the potatoes and the leeks, which seemed so exciting with their green and white spears. Then I made the error of thinking: why not save a pot? So in they both went together and bubbled away, as the water grew misty. The eggs I had learned to do "easy over". That gesture, too, of not breaking the yoke seemed a marvelous discovery. I must have been quite oblivious, a dream-filled Don Quixote, charging ahead. To make a long story short, I put the leaks on a blue plate, and arranged the potatoes, looking like slightly gray stones, next to them. I put the eggs with their shriveled yellow eyes, off to the side and sat down with my man to eat. The first slash of the knife through the glade of green stalk released a river of mud that rushed out and covered the eggs, and swirled around the potatoes. The meal rested under a flood of doom.

Of course I cried. And the young man said it didn't matter. But it did, and because we never talked about it, too much will continued in the way we approached each other, as if the worst meal of breakfast still had the power of a curse. Respect for food, its simple equation of human affection, the inclusion of all frailty, waited for better times, for Italy, for accepting a different, more challenging definition of starvation.

# Honeymoon Dinner on Mahabaleshwar Mountain

*Victor Rangel-Ribeiro*

Because I had joined the advertising giant J. Walter Thompson in Bombay scant months before our wedding in September 1954, and been granted just a week's leave, Lea and I had planned to spend our honeymoon holed up in our cozy apartment in that city; but a cousin (whom I will not name!) discovered we were in town. Even in those pre-Twitter pre-Facebook days she managed to share her discovery with assorted aunts, uncles, and several hundred first and second cousins, who then felt duty-bound to stop by and share our happiness. Moved to tears by so much affection, two days into the honeymoon we decided to escape from the city and flee to the hills.

Our choice was Mahabaleshwar, the fabled hill station 4,000 feet up in the Sahyadri range, just a crow's flight from Bombay but a couple of hundred miles by road. We were told that hotels there closed down during the monsoon, and did not open until early October, but we found one that was almost closed and had not yet quite reopened that still agreed to take us. A fast morning train rushed us to Poona, whooshing through countless tunnels as it climbed up the Western Ghats; arriving there in mid-afternoon, we took a minibus to our destination, still another seventy miles away. Our dozen or so fellow passengers were a mixed bunch; some spoke only Marathi, a language akin to Konkani that Lea and I, being from Goa, could understand but not speak, while others spoke Hindustani and Hindi, which we had no trouble speaking, and yet others also spoke English. Conversations flowed smoothly back and forth multilingually until, in an hour, we came to the first big ghat or mountain, when our driver began to treat our bus the way cowboys ride their horses in movies when pursued by howling "Apaches". His exhilaration grew as the mountains became progressively steeper, the road narrower, and the potholes both deeper and more numerous; each time a passenger debarked we wondered whether the man had really reached his destination or gotten off in fear of losing his life. Lea and I were the only passengers left when the bus pulled into Mahabaleshwar and dropped us off at our hotel. In hopes of receiving a larger baksheesh, our driver reminded us that he had taken us safely through miles and miles of exquisite scenery; we were quite surprised by this, being both convinced it had consisted solely of precipices luring us to our death on one side and rock faces daring us to try a collision on the other.

The hotel, quite clean and comfortable, was also quite empty; the man who greeted us warmly and showed us to our room turned out later to be reception clerk, manager, and maitre d' all rolled into one. He suggested that, as we still had about an hour of sunlight left, we might want to go take a look at Bombay Point, from where— though twilight was already creeping on to the valley—we could get a good look at... Bombay. With a tout as guide, we agreed to go look longingly at a city from which we had run away just hours earlier. By the time we reached the point a drizzle had intensified, fog had settled on the valley, and we saw not a thing.

As a life-long lover of music, I owe a depth of gratitude to Johann Sebastian Bach for having died when he did. Had he not picked July 28, 1750, to be his last day on earth, All-India Radio would not have organized a studio concert in 1950 to celebrate his two-hundredth death anniversary, and another broadcast a month later. Scores in hand and critical antennae quivering, I attended both events as music critic for Bombay's National and Sunday Standards.

The second time, alas, instead of focusing on the performance, my attention was riveted on a young woman who was turning pages for the pianist. Struck both by her beauty and her total absorption in the music, I looked for her, in vain, at every subsequent concert I attended. And then one day, after I had written several times about a young Bombay violinist who was concertizing in Europe, the young man's father invited me to dinner at his home. I rang the doorbell. She answered the door. I remember not a thing about what was served that night, but it must have been good; I remember going back time after time for more of her mother's cooking.

For the next four years I wooed Lea with a passion. Stitching together snatches of free time from work, I waylaid her to and from her music lessons. I sustained myself through all the pain of lugging her heavy music books around by keeping my ultimate goal in mind—marriage. To those people who later called me a cradle snatcher, let me put the matter in perspective: would they have called me that, had I been 84, and she 76? That's how old we are now, and we had the same eight-year difference between us when I was 24 and she 16.

In all the years that I chased Lea all over Bombay, I never doubted that I would eventually marry her; she, to my chagrin, held diametrically opposing views. Oh, she was glad enough to have me along as a perambulating caddy for her music, but marriage loomed nowhere on her horizon. On one historic bus ride, during which she heard the 250th declaration of love on my part, she took my bus ticket and wrote on the back of it: Victor Rangel-Ribeiro, I will never NEVER NEVER marry you. She signed and dated it November 11th, 1952.

Pointing out that any two negatives taken together make a positive, I tried to turn this into a "Gotcha!" moment; she retorted that that was why she had written not two "nevers" but three. Desperate times call for desperate measures. Before tucking the ticket away in my wallet, I made her this prophesy: "Not only will you marry me, but Bishop Gracias will be made the first Indian Cardinal ever, so he can marry us."

Tall order, for in British India the top Roman Catholic prelate had to be a white man. Thus, in Bombay, we had Cardinal Roberts, a Brit; Bishop Valerian Gracias, a Goan like me, stood permanently in his shadow. Big problem! How was I going to keep my promise and make Gracias a cardinal, when, even if Roberts were "removed" with extreme prejudice, another Brit would take his place?

Some historians have claimed that, once India got rid of the British, Cardinal Roberts automatically became a shoo-out and Bishop Gracias a shoo-in; for these ill-informed purveyors of perverted history, after 1947 it was only a waiting game. The truth lies elsewhere; having waited far too long already, I decided to take a trip to Rome and force the papal hand. I figured that my best bet to get past the gauntlet of cardinals and Swiss Guards would be for me to go disguised as a cardinal, since cardinals come in large as well as small and irregular sizes, and Swiss Guards all look the same. It worked: A kindly but frail old cardinal accompanied me to the papal chamber; once I was face to face with His Holiness, I played my master card, calling out loudly, "Holy Father, please hear my confession!"

The pope waved the group back and motioned me to kneel beside his throne. Ah, blessed privacy in plain view!

As he leaned his ear towards me, I whispered, "Most Holy Father, the first sin I must confess is that I am not a cardinal."

He whispered back, "My son, I knew that already. Security tipped me off."

"They did?"

"That old cardinal who walked in with you, his arm around your shoulder and leaning on you for support, that's Antonio*, head

*Antonio Mangiabene (b. Perugia, 1913, d. Milano 1975). Son of a potato farmer. Master of disguises, had distinguished career in Swiss Guards, until summary dismissal Dec. 12, 1952 for escorting unauthorized foreign visitor into the papal presence. Heartbroken; suicide attempt in St. Peter's Square failed as he tried difficult task of falling on his halberd. [WikiMedia. Further corroboration needed.]

of security detail. He not only had you under surveillance, he had you in his grip. He let you go when I gave him the secret sign."

"I apologize for the brash deception," I said. "But I am desperate, and have a most urgent request to make of Your Holiness. Please make Bishop Gracias a cardinal."

"My child, your Prime Minister Nehru calls me every day with the same demand. I give him the same answer I'm giving you now, 'I'll think about it'. There's no hurry! In keeping with the ageless vision of Our Holy Mother the Church, I tend to think in terms of millennia rather than a few paltry years."

"Holy Father," I said quickly, "I beg you to accelerate your thinking: I have more clout than Mr. Nehru."

Surprised, he leaned closer. "How so?"

"I have friends in low places."

"My child, 'low' is a relative term. How low is your low?"

He winked at security; I had to be quick. "Holy Father, as low as your two kneecaps."

Was that a hint of fear I saw in those suddenly widened eyes? The pope waved security away; when he scratched his right ear, his Secretary of State promptly approached and knelt beside me. "I'm making Gracias in Bombay a cardinal," His Holiness told him, "and I'm doing it presto agitato. Call a consistory for a month from tomorrow, and make sure you have a cardinal's robe long enough to fit him. He's a very tall man."

Both the pope and his secretary of state have long since passed away, so you'll have to take my word for it that this indeed is a true account of what happened that day. Have faith: I have an honest face! Besides, Church records will confirm that Valerian Gracias was elevated to the rank of cardinal at a consistory held in Rome on January 12, 1953, exactly two months and a day after I had made my prophesy to Lea, and exactly a month after my meeting with the pope; they will also reveal that on September 18, 1954, the cardinal celebrated a wedding mass at the Pro-Cathedral of the Holy Name in

Bombay, only the second such since his investiture. Having reached the point in the ceremony where I had assured him that I, Victor Rangel hyphen Ribeiro, being of sound mind, did hereby take the beauteous Lea Vaz as my lawful wedded wife, to have and to hold, in sickness and in etc., he turned to Lea, and began, "Do you, Lea Vaz —"

Forgetting she had said she would never marry me, Lea impulsively cut the question short, saying, "I do."

Whereupon this tall, tall man leaned over and gently said to her, "Not yet, my child."

You won't have to call the Vatican to check on the truth of this anecdote; Lea has told the story herself, many times.

It took Lea and me less time to get back to our hotel in Mahabaleshwar than it had taken us to walk to Bombay Point, because now we were fairly running to beat the rain. The clerk announced dinner would be served at eight-thirty, which gave us time to change out of our wet clothes and gave him time to morph into maitre d'. Our waiter turned out to be a tall, huskily built soccer player who had just come back from a game, and still had his football cleats on, a fact that bothered him not in the least. The menu listed several mouth-watering dishes, but before we could waste any time making a choice, the maitre d' informed us that, this being the off-season, the larder was bare; so bare, that we had no choice of entrée. Our hearts sank. But when he told us it would be roast chicken and baked potatoes, with the soup du jour, wine and dessert, we were delighted. Roast chicken? Baked potatoes? Bring them on!

Fifteen minutes later, we saw our waiter come out of the kitchen bearing our meal. We unfolded our napkins. I looked long and deep into Lea's eyes. I held her hand. I murmured, "I love you."

And then the hotel's doorbell rang, and the maitre d', assuming the role of manager, motioned to our waiter to set his tray down on a nearby table and answer the door.

From outside the dining room we heard the murmur of voices. The waiter came back and whispered in the manager's ear; both of them went back into the foyer. When the manager returned, he explained that a couple with a grown son and daughter had taken a chance and come to Mahabaleshwar without making any reservations; and since the only other hotel still open had refused to take them in, he could not turn them out into the dark chilly night. We gathered that if he had done so, they would have been immediately set upon by a pack of jackals. Or just a prowling tiger.

Of course we agreed he had done the right thing. We also agreed that the newcomers could share our table with us.

Our manager switched roles once again and flipped his fingers at the waiter; impassively, that worthy picked up our chicken and took it back into the kitchen. That was when we first began to suspect that it's true what people say: no good deed really goes unpunished.

So three days and approximately two hours after Lea uttered her premature but memorable "I do" at the Pro-Cathedral, she and I are at the hotel in Mahabaleshwar, still waiting for our dinner as the clock's hands creep past nine. We have been moved to a larger table. Our four fellow guests turn out to be impressively large, and all of them admit to being ravenously hungry. "This is one dinner I'm looking forward to," the father says, patting his stomach. "It's been a long day." It surely has.

Then we hear the clicking of metal cleats on hard wooden boards and the kitchen door opens and our waiter comes in, beaming, bearing a larger tray triumphantly aloft. He has good reason to be pleased: There will be food enough for the six of us, after all.

I should state here that Indian chickens are so small they would be routinely classed as "large" in any American supermarket, but though the tray still holds only one small chicken and some watered down soup, the chef has pulled off a gastronomical miracle of quasi-biblical proportions: the potatoes have increased, and multiplied. True, thanks to the fact that the older couple are served first, Lea and I get to eat less than two ounces of chicken apiece, but the waiter piles enough potatoes on our plates to provide us with a lifetime of memories.

# The Duchess Flounder

*Peter Selgin*

Around this time you met Angie. You'd gone into a tavern named Squirrels for a beer (paid for with emergency money sent by your parents) and to write in your journal. You were tired. You hadn't slept very much the night before. You hadn't been feeling well.   Something to do with your gut. You were in a lousy mood, too. You remembered—the last time you saw each other—having lent Jack Ajax ten dollars that he'd promised to repay you when you rendezvoused in Corvallis. Now you're sure you'll never see Ajax again. It's not the ten dollars that bothers you so much, it's the thought of having been taken advantage of, the sense of betrayal. You conjure a scene in your journal where you find him bent over a cue stick in the pool hall upstairs. Shhh, he says when confronted by you. This is a very tough shot I'm trying to make here. Don't blow it for me.

That's when you grab him by the shirt collar, pull his nose to your chin and call him a greasy, no-good, mooching bum, and push him to the floor.

Someone taps your shoulder. A woman stands there asking if you're okay. You were fast asleep, she says. Either that or you were resting with your head in your beer.

She askes if she can join you. She has short dark hair and the face of a homecoming queen, circa 1962. She says she plays the piano, enjoys clog dancing, sees a chiropractor once a week, and likes meeting new people. She asks where you're from and where you're staying. You tell her about your psychotic room.

Show me, she says.

You walk her through the dark across Central Park to the Ghetto and show her. She seems impressed. Whoever lived here before must have had quite an interesting personality, she says. She sees your guitar in the corner.

That yours? You nod. Play me something, she says.

She smoothes your bedcovers and sits with her arms folded expectantly, waiting as you tune your guitar. You play her one of your songs, one with a Spanish lilt to it that begins, *There's so much left to be said / that will never be said / because it's been said too often.* When you finish she says, It doesn't make a lot of sense. But that's okay. It strikes you then that she's odd, that normal people don't go around telling other people what they really think of their songs. You wonder, too, if she's come to get laid or be serenaded or both, but anyway you're too drunk and tired for sex, so you play her two or three more songs. Then she stands up, straightens her skirt, and says, I live about an hour north of here, in Salem. She writes her phone number down. Give me a call tomorrow, why don't you?

When the time comes the next day having no phone of your own you use a public payphone. It's your first encounter with Pacific Northwest payphones. Unlike phones back East, where the operator cuts into long-distance calls to ask you for your money, in Oregon they let you finish your call, and then, after you hang up, the phone rings and a friendly voice says, *Please deposit an additional ---- cents for the past ---- minutes.* This astonishes you. They are so trusting, these people, these Oregonians: how can you possibly take advantage and not pay? When you get through to Angie she says she has a busy schedule that day, clogging lessons, a violin concerto, a meeting with her lawyer to finalize her divorce papers. She hopes to spend a 'mellow evening' and 'get to sleep early.' You say that sounds fine by you. She gives you directions. You'll hitchhike up Interstate 5 and get there hopefully by seven, in time for dinner.

You meet Angie at Bush Park Memorial, where you watch a group of Serbo-Croatian folk dancers. She asks you if you're into jitterbugging. I've never been that much of a dancer, you tell her. Then I'll have to teach you, she says. She suggests that you both go out dancing after dinner. She knows some good places.

On the way to her home you stop at a bar for a beer. Angie isn't talkative. You ask her about her family. All of her closest relatives, those who haven't committed suicide, are insane, apparently. When you ask her to elaborate, she says, Don't ask so many questions. After a silence she adds, I don't really like people that talk too much.

You say, I appreciate that.

You do seem to talk quite a lot, she says. Do I? Yes, she says, you do. I've never thought of myself as a big talker, you say. Well you are. And you're disagreeable, too. I *am*? (You hadn't noticed that you were especially disagreeable, either.) You're disagreeing with me right now, she says. Really? You certainly are; don't you hear yourself? You come right out and say what you think, don't you? you say. I don't like beating around the bush. Do you have a problem with that? No, no. I hate having my bush beaten around. What's that supposed to mean? *It was attempting humor, however feebly.* And that's another thing, I really don't care for your sense of humor. It reminds me of your songs. I didn't get them, either. *Well, different people have different sensibilities, I guess.* If you're going to talk to people, you should say things they understand, otherwise don't say anything. *Yes, I think that's a very good idea.* I'm tired. I don't feel like dancing. Let's just have dinner. Okay?

But first Angie drives you to her place, a small apartment in a run-down shack of a building. There's an ironing board in the middle of the living room, with copies of *Readers Digest* tossed around. A case of books. *A Divorced Woman's Guide to Being Single, Living Alone and Loving It, The Secret Powers of EST.* You're suddenly ill at ease. She hands you a phone book. Why don't you make us reservations. You name the restaurant and I'll tell you if it's any good. While you look through the phone book she takes a pair of slacks off her couch and starts ironing them. As she irons you rattle off the names of a dozen restaurants, to each of which she says Nope, or, Uh-uh. You name every restaurant in Salem. Try Stephnyville, she says, folding another pair of slacks and starting on a negligee. There's supposed to be a good seafood place there.

An hour later she drives you down a series of foggy, narrow roads to The Duchess Flounder, or some such place, with a swinging fat neon sign saying SEAFOOD and where the hostess, an elderly woman in a flowery dress, seats you in what she calls the 'lounge' to wait for a table.

Why don't you pay for the drinks, Angie says while you wait. I'll take care of dinner, since I know you don't have much money. She orders a cocktail; you order a glass of house Chablis. By the time you get a table she's had two whiskey sours. For her main course she orders the most expensive item on the menu, the Captain's Platter. You settle for scrod. Your date hardly says a word while cracking crab legs and lobster claws, tearing their insides out with her teeth, dipping them in melted butter with pointy fingers. As she lifts them to her mouth the seafood chunks drip butter on her bib.

Through the whole meal she doesn't say a word. Meanwhile the pile of cracked shells mounts on her plate, a dada study in moribund grays and pinks. Done, she daubs her little mouth with her napkin and finishes her fourth or fifth cocktail. Mmm, she says, tossing back the dregs. I am so stuffed, and works her mouth to loosen trapped food particles. Aren't you stuffed? I'm stuffed. I couldn't dance if I wanted to. She leans back in the booth, rubs her belly, daubs her lips again. She reminds you of a praying mantis that has just finished eating its mate. As a matter of fact, she says, I think I'd like to just go home now. Do you mind? She asks the waitress for the check. When it comes she hands it to you, saying, Why don't you get this one? Our next date'll be on me—how does that sound? I mean, a

116

man should pay for the first date. It's only fair, right?

Back at her place she starts ironing again. I'm awfully tired, she says, putting a pleat in a pair of slacks. Aren't you tired? You must be tired. Why don't you find out when the next bus for Corvallis is?

You tell her the next bus for Corvallis is at three in the morning. Supposing I just sleep on your couch? you say.

Oh, no: not on the first date. Sorry. I'll stay up and iron until it's time. Sound okay to you?

Three hours, a pile of laundry, and four *Reader's Digests* later, Angie drops you off at the Greyhound depot. You stand there with your guitar watching as she drives off through the fog. The bus leaves in an hour. You sit on the curb stroking your guitar as older couples emerge from the Coach Room Bar & Grill next door, dropping quarters into your case as they stumble past.

# Firsts & Seconds

## R.A. Rycraft

The best worst meal essay should probably begin with a family. My family. My used-to-be family. Not that I don't have family anymore. I do. Lots of family. Most of which is made up of members from *that* family. But we are no longer *that* family, in *that* context, in *that* particular time. Anyway, the best worst meal essay is about *that* used-to-be family. And that used-to-be family is sitting down at one of my used-to-be favorite restaurants—Rockin' Baja Lobster—with my first used-to-be husband and his not-quite-my-friend-yet wife.

See, here's the thing. Divorce number one was nasty. But there were our two little kids: Casi and Kevin, four and five when the divorce was final. So over the years, as anger finally gave way to apathy, and since both of us had remarried, there was a need to collaborate in order to create some sort of civil place where four parents could be in the same room at birthdays and holidays—a civil place where four parents could cooperate to raise two kids. First used-to-be husband and his not-quite-my-friend-yet wife worked harder than I to be civil. No. More than that. They worked harder to be pleasant—even *friendly*. Actually, it was clear that not-quite-my-friend-yet wanted to build a relationship with me. I was not exactly thrilled about the prospect since being civil was about all I could muster. Friends? I thought not. But not-quite-my-friend-yet has a couple of strong character traits—persistence and patience. I believe it is entirely possible that the moment she agreed to marry my first used-to-be husband and take on his two kids every other weekend and on holidays, she developed and executed a plan of attack on me that lasted years. She'd make a point to sit and talk with me at every one of "our" son Kevin's Little League and soccer games or "our" daughter Casi's choir concerts and dance recitals. She'd send little notes out of the blue just to say, "Hi. I'm thinking about you." And the kicker? She began inviting us to dinner. It took a few tries, but, like I said, that woman is nothing if not persistent, and I finally said "Yes" just to get her off my back.

Now, don't go thinking the dinner thing was an instant success and that everybody got along and felt comfortable. That was hardly the case. In fact, let's just say that it took years to work out the kinks. The conversation was often stilted and the meals were often tense. At least at the kids' activities, if conversation lagged there were kids to watch. But in a restaurant? Where the *modus operandi* is eat, drink, and talk? All I can say is that by the time we met for dinner at Rockin' Baja Lobster, I was glad to have four gabby kids. In addition to Casi (18) and Kevin (17), there were now two more kids in my family—Michael (11) and Tricia (9)—who could be depended on to dominate dinner discussion regardless of the occasion or place. None of my kids ever understood the concept of being seen not heard—well, except for kid number three, but that's another story—sort of. Michael is a lot like his dad (my second husband), which means he is kind and generous as well as sensitive and vulnerable. But it also means that he doesn't say much, holds his tongue a lot, and isn't very demonstrative.

Which brings me to husband number two.

Back at Rockin' Baja Lobster, we are devouring warm tortillas smeared with whipped honey and chili butter. My second husband is sitting between me and our youngest daughter, Tricia. I am sitting next to not-quite-my-friend-yet and conversation is focused on "our" son Kevin being accepted into University of Nevada, Las Vegas' Criminal Justice program (we don't yet know that he will dump the college idea and join the Air Force), and my first year as a returning student at California State University, San Marcos. She mentions her promotion to branch manager at Home Savings and

Loan. "Our" daughter Casi tells us about her job as an Emergency Medical Technician (EMT) at Bowers Ambulance. First used-to-be husband brings up classic cars, which puts a damper on all other conversation. But that doesn't matter because first used-to-be husband wants to talk, and he has learned that nothing interests my second husband more than talking about cars—classic cars—and to be even more specific—classic Porsches.

My second husband can talk about cars exhaustively and in elaborate, minute detail. The only other thing he talks about more than cars is work. He's an Emergency Room nurse. That, too, he can discuss exhaustively and in elaborate, minute detail. Now, try to get him to talk about some kind of problem with the kids or some kind of friction between the two of us—then there's little to say. Like the time Kevin took a pocket knife to school, loaned it to a friend, who threatened a girl with the knife before giving it back and Kevin was expelled for the remainder of the school year. Or the time I got so frustrated helping Michael with homework (because helping Michael with homework always involved several hours), and I was getting louder and louder and more and more angry and closer and closer to smacking the kid—all of this within earshot—and my second husband did not intervene to rescue Michael or to rescue me. Or the time Casi told me she had sex with a guy from church, and I bought a pregnancy test. And, lo, the little plus sign was pink. Casi was sixteen. Or the time Tricia—very upset because Casi was pregnant and the baby's father was making life difficult for Casi and, by extension, the rest of us—wanted to know why her life had to change just because Casi was having a baby. This from a girl who was seven at the time. Or the night the guy next door shot his wife and little girl before calling 911 and committing suicide on the line, and I thought we've got to strategize a way to talk to the kids about how their friend's dad murdered her and her mom—their babysitter—and make our kids feel safe. What do you do with all that? Alone? Without help? Without input? Without a husband or father with anything to say? As my second husband once put it,

"When I hear something worth talking about, I'll talk."

When the Rockin' Baja food arrives, it arrives in buckets. Literally. Three of them. The buckets are full to overflowing with crab legs, langostinos, lobster tails, shrimp, carne asada, and grilled chicken. Conversation halts. We don't stand on ceremony at Rockin' Baja Lobster. It doesn't matter who is present, including first used-to-be husband and not-quite-my-friend-yet wife. There is no polite passing of the buckets around the table. It's every person for him or herself. This is finger food, and we put our fingers to work, lunging for the buckets, digging in and grabbing our favorite shellfish, ignoring the steak and chicken. We suck Cajun seasoning off the shells. We suck those shells dry. We strip shrimp. We crack crab. We tear open lobster tails. Once inside—we pick out the meat—every single tender, white morsel. We shove the succulent stuff into our mouths. We swipe at our chins, lick our fingers, smack our lips. All of us are in flavor heaven, and the company seems pretty good, too.

But as it happens, nine-year-old Tricia eats more shrimp than anyone else. And as it also happens, Tricia reacts to shrimp. I hesitate to call it an allergic reaction because now, as an adult, she can eat all the shrimp she wants with no reaction at all. But on this day, thirteen years ago, Tricia has a reaction. It's the same reaction she's had for years: Eat shrimp; throw up. Tricia is warned not to eat shrimp. I warn her. Her father warns her. But Tricia loves shrimp more than anything and understands that if she eats it she will suffer consequences. She cannot help herself. The temptation is too great. Those three buckets of shrimp represent a form of torture for a child who would rather throw up than deny herself the sensual taste bud adventure of eating as much shrimp as she can stand before the inevitable urge drives her out of her chair and into a mad rush for the bathroom. To be honest, I didn't notice her eating the shrimp. Her father must not have noticed either, or he would have said something sooner. But when she jumps up from the table to run for the bathroom, he has plenty to say, and he says it loud, and he says it mean, and he says it in front of first used-to-be-husband and his not-quite-my-friend-yet wife.

Now there is a history here. I tend to be passionate about a lot of things. I am incapable of *feeling* in a steady, unexcitable way. I am demonstrative. Sometimes that's a good thing, sometimes not. And in that used-to-be-family, in that faraway time, it was often not a good thing. My passionate nature partnered with my second husband's *dis*passionate nature proved . . . difficult. When frustrated and angry, I raised my voice and yelled. The kids affectionately refer to those times as Mom's *flip-out fits*. But they will also be the first to tell you—if Mom goes silent, get out of her way.

My second husband was adept at prompting flip-out fits. All he had to do was remain silent. It was his right. He would rather die a thousand deaths than give up his silence to engage in a serious we-need-to-figure-this-out discussion with me. And the more silent he remained, the more frustrated I grew. That silence was crazy-making. It made me yell louder, made me grow meaner, made me say whatever I could think to say, regardless of how horrible or nasty, just to get him to respond. That silence reduced me to a foot stomping, door slamming, object-throwing, screaming banshee. It was as though engaging in any sort of discussion, whether civil or heated, was against his inter-personal relationship code, as if answering questions or problem-solving family challenges was a sign of weakness rather than strength. He wore that silence like a carapace of honor, a carapace of courage. And that carapace had a face—it was emotionless and *dead*.

But that was my second husband's M.O. *then*: his M.O. *at home* I should say. At family gatherings or dinner with friends? When it was *much less* likely I'd raise my voice or pick a fight? Well, that was another story. That was when his code changed. That was when *he* picked fights with *me*, humiliated me, the kids—or went ballistic on all of us. For fourteen years of marriage it was the same story.

Home—silence. Public—dress-em-down like a Drill Sergeant.

At Rockin' Baja Lobster, Tricia is dressed-down for eating shrimp. Now this is a kid who knows how to get what she wants, but when she gets in trouble, she is crushed that you are mad at her—and the crushed thing is no act. It's as if the action and negative consequence stuff does not compute. When she was five years old and wanted ice cream from the ice cream truck? She got in my purse, took a twenty, stopped the truck, bought ice cream for all of her friends, and brought me the change. Imagine her heatbreak when I scolded her. On this day, at Rockin' Baja Lobster, her father yells at her for eating the shrimp. He does not allow her to go to the bathroom. She sits back down, bursts into tears, and throws up. There is an audible gasp throughout the dining room. Meals are ruined. A lot of them. Rockin' Baja Lobster is a busy place. I am horrified.

Well, maybe not. To be horrified, I would need to feel. I look at my second husband and feel . . . nothing . . . except a snap of emotional deadness that is almost physical in its intensity.

I stand up, put my finger in his face and very quietly I say, "Never again."

He grumbles something back. I hear him, but I don't listen. I tune him out. I move on. Not-quite-my-friend-yet grabs all the napkins within reach and begins to wipe the table. The waitress rushes toward us with towels. I am beside Tricia. I mop her up. I tell her it's okay. Everything will be okay. But, of course, it is not okay. Silence at the table is palpable—uncomfortable—unforgettable. I comfort Tricia, but I, too, am silent.

This is not the first time I have gone silent on my second husband. But it is the last. And what is most miserable about my silence on *this* day during *that* meal at Rockin' Baja Lobster—in the presence of my children, first used-to-be husband, and his not-quite-my-friend-yet-wife—is that it marks the end of my second marriage as well as the end of that used-to-be family.

# The Best They Had To Offer

*Rick Mulkey*

In truth, I had planned to write that I'd never had a bad meal. As anyone who knows me will tell you, I like food. It isn't even a matter of liking to eat--though I do. I enjoy the pleasures of food. I enjoy the experience of food, the anticipation, the ritual. Dreaming of the complex scents and tastes of even a simple dish of eggs with tomatoes and bacon can wake me in the middle of the night. As a child I grew up with a multitude of food smells in the house. Though not poor, my family was far from wealthy. We lived in a rural, small town and my mother and father raised a great deal of our food. There was a large garden, nearly an acre in size, with every imaginable vegetable. Often, on my grandparent's nearby farm, my parents would raise a beef steer, a couple of hogs, and dozens of chickens and guinea fowl. In fact, we often incubated and hatched the baby chickens in the basement of our home before taking them off to the farm. Throughout summer and early fall the smell of jams and jellies rose in the steam from the stove where they bubbled and cooked before being canned, and the pungent, acidic aroma of cucumbers and cabbages pickling in a large ceramic crock nestled in the corner of the kitchen, lingered in the house long after they had been preserved and stored on shelves in the darkest corner of the basement. Though I may not have been able to express it as a small boy, the systems and patterns my family had in place around food brought me as much comfort as the food itself.

Most mornings I woke to fresh eggs gathered the day before

from the chicken coup. They fried in bacon grease. On Sundays we ate a fat hen whose neck my father had wrung and whose body my mother had cleaned and feathered. In autumn the smell of garlic and canned tomatoes simmered with a roast from the side of beef, or even better, the sausages my parents made after they slaughtered the hog sizzled and popped in a cast iron pan. Everything was used, from the lard kept in the pantry, to the pickled pigs feet my parents ate as a snack late at night. My parents worked hard, long hours, and had little of their own, at least in the way most of us would now measure financial success. And I remember I often thought of us as always having less than many of my school friends, but in fact, I now realize, we had a great abundance. More than I could have appreciated or understood then, or even as a young man.

In Poland in the summer of 1992, only a few years after Eastern Europe had opened its doors to the West, my wife, Susan, and I taught at a language college in Warsaw. At this time, I still didn't understand abundance or want. Yet, I'm sure that Zbigniew and his wife Danuta, our hosts in Warsaw, believed they were sharing something of their own abundance with us. We were staying with them while studying Polish language and culture before our teaching jobs started. Zbigniew had been a relatively successful communist physician, but now, in the fledgling stages of Polish capitalism he found himself working with an ambulance crew. A better job than many, but not what he had been in his previous life, during what Susan and I were sure Zbigniew saw as the good old days of communism. Still, he wanted to show us that Poland was not a poor country, and that he and his family were in no need of help from the West. Dinners each evening were filled with lots of meats, usually sausage, but often chicken (far more expensive than sausage), and even once, for what was a special occasion, an aspic that Danuta had made from the fats she saved over several weeks. There were also plenty of fresh vegetables from their own garden and cherries from the tree in the back yard. Though most Americans would have found it pretty simple fair, it was clearly more than simple to Zbigniew and Danuta.

Yet, it was a very simple meal that ended up being what I have thought of for most of my adult life as the worst meal I've eaten. It was a breakfast eaten quickly the morning Susan and I were traveling to Auschwitz. We had an early express train ride into Krakow, then we planned a bus ride to Auschwitz. I'm sure Zbigniew meant only the best when the night before the trip he set out several frankfurters, or parowka, as he called them, with the heavy, dense bread that had become a staple of our meals in Poland, and fresh butter. We woke. I ate the wieners while my wife stuck to eating the bread and butter. We thought little of the meal, then headed to the city center to catch our train.

In general I had liked the food in Poland. I saw the heavily creamed herring, the fat-ribboned sausages, and the gelatinized meat products slathered on brown bread as part of the adventure of living in post-communist Eastern Europe. The food was dissimilar enough from what I had known to seem exotic, yet familiar enough to seem comforting. As long as I stayed away from foods meant to appeal to American tourists such as the street vendors' pizza made with ketchup rather than sauce and a cheese far more similar to muenster than mozzarella, then I'd been okay. Yes, I had worried some when a Polish colleague offered me pork for lunch one day from a roast that had rested uncovered on the windowsill for a day and a night. But I managed to eat the meal with little more than a couple of lower intestinal rumbles of disagreement. I certainly wouldn't have expected any more than this from a couple of wieners.

We had been on the train less than an hour when I started to feel sick. To save money we always purchased third class seats. This meant little room and more people than seats. Fortunately we had seats. Unfortunately my seat was across from an old Ukrainian woman carrying a half dozen bags and satchels filled with every imaginable sausage. The smell of the kielbasa rising through the cramped compartment made me dizzy. "I have to get some air," I whispered to Susan, and left to stand in the doorway.

By the time we arrived in Krakow and caught our bus I suspected the frankfurters. By the time we entered the Auschwitz museum beneath the infamous sign, "Work Brings Freedom," I could hardly stand up straight. I don't know if the horrors of the museum, the glass encased rooms of human hair, gold fillings from teeth, the piled suitcases, including one with the family name of one of our closest friends, or the way the young German boy, also a tourist, seemed to wander from room to room unmoved by what he saw, made me feel worse, but I became sicker and sicker, having to stop every few minutes. In the hotel that night, bent over a Polish toilet, I blamed Zbigniew for leaving the meat out all night; I blamed Poland for its poverty; I blamed myself for bringing us to this part of the world. But by morning, with the worst of it over, we sat in a small café in the Stary Miasto, the Old Town, listening to church bells and drinking iced coffee.

Back in Warsaw, things were never the same, however, with Zbigniew and Danuta. I ate little of what they provided us during those last couple of weeks. Most nights I chose to go out with friends, and by the end of our stay with them, we'd had little to say.

For years after, I imagined that truly was the worst meal I had ever eaten. I often told people how I'd been taken down by a lowly hot dog. Recently, however, I've started to realize that for Zbigniew it was more upsetting than I could have understood. For him, he was providing me with food and hospitality. It said something of who he and his family were. There was ritual in the way Danuta placed the food on the table each evening, the way bread was piled on the plate, the tomato salted, the dark, fatty sausages sliced and fanned out across the platter. It was abundance they were sharing with me, a symbol of who and what they were, and I was too young, too spoiled, perhaps, to realize it. For Zbigniew it was not meant as a worst meal. In fact, I've come to understand what a sacrifice it was for him and his family to host us and to provide for us. These meals were always the best they had to offer.

Certainly there are meals that are better than others. There are even meals we want to forget and do forget. We all have had them at someone's home, or at a restaurant, or even made them ourselves. But there is always a moment, or a flavor, or a presentation that is remarkable about a meal, any meal. Whether it is carving a holiday bird, or preparing that casserole from Great Grandma's recipe, as long as some ritual is involved, a sense of community and sharing, then even the worst meal is worth savoring.

# "Sukiyaki Song"

*Alexandra Marshall*

"Well, it was definitely *my* Worst Meal," my daughter says to this day about my Best Intentioned dinner suggestion— Most Expensive too—at Tokyo's New Otani Hotel.

While backpacking on a budget in Asia she'd been eating Pad Thai twice a day for the previous few weeks, and though Sukiyaki wasn't her idea of comfort food—her preferred diet was the boxed macaroni and cheese I'd packed in my suitcase for the next leg of her journey—when I mentioned that the cozy pleasure of tissue-thin beef cooked at the table had been my own introduction to Japanese cuisine, this seemed like a sufficiently convincing endorsement. I didn't yet realize that to save money and guard against digestive distress she'd been avoiding meat altogether, though in a four-star hotel in the "Garden of Asia," wasn't Sukiyaki the foolproof entry-level meal?

I hadn't actually eaten it in decades, having learned to favor more exotic alternatives during a stay of several months in Kyoto and while working at the Japanese Consulate back in New York. In meeting up with my daughter at that point in her journey I was returning to Japan for the first time in more than 35 years, and I was eager to share my love of that culture while providing R&R in a country considered too costly for backpackers. Her introduction to Tokyo was to be a splurge, and I'd chosen this luxury hotel for two reasons. It has a 400 year-old 10-acre garden that even includes a waterfall, and because I was fortunate enough to have stayed there once before, as an overnight guest of Japanese friends, back when it was called The New Otani because it was new.

The precision of this overlap was fitting because I too had set out after college graduation with a round-the-world air ticket valid for a year. I'd made an unexpectedly committed first stop to study Japanese classical dance in Kyoto, so it was the faster-moving second half of my journey inspiring my daughter when she announced her intention to embark upon a comparable adventure.

Times had changed, of course, and while it definitely took guts for my provincial parents to send me off in the summer of 1965 with only the promise of a trail of airmailed letters to keep them informed of my whereabouts, our daughter's senior year had commenced with the September 11th attacks. The world I had ventured into took kindly to Americans in that precious interval between JFK's assassination and the still gradually escalating war in Vietnam, but in the shadow of the radically transformative events of 2001, I don't mind admitting that, only months later, it wasn't easy to watch her disappear onto a plane with her American passport. I felt responsible for having set such a benign—naïve—example with my own improvised itinerary back when I don't even remember my parents having to say, "Be careful."

But during the summer and fall our temperamentally cautious daughter had proved steadily reassuring with frequent email updates and occasional phone contact—her international mobile worked everywhere but Kenya—so it wasn't until the horrific Bali nightclub bombings on October 12th that our worst fears took specific form. Her most recent call from the porch hammock of a beach bungalow on the Thai island of Koh Peng Yang had featured a vivid description of the fluid community of travelers like her who were coming from or going on to Kuta, the tourist-friendly Balinese beach counterpart where the bombings occurred. Until we were able to verify that she hadn't decided to make a spontaneous detour to nearby Indonesia, it was frighteningly easy to imagine her among the targeted foreign nationals—240 injured and 202 dead—whose young lives were taken that Saturday night.

Those casualties were still being counted a dozen days later when we each flew into Narita Airport, I on Northwest from the States and she on Air Cathay Pacific from Hong Kong. She was scheduled to land just ahead of me, so we'd agreed to meet up in the common baggage claim area, a plan excluding consideration of the fact that, under heightened security, any lingering passenger would be regarded with suspicion for not briskly moving along with the others. My flight arrived after a significant enough delay that, as I finally descended the long escalator into the baggage hall—she at the bottom wearing a girlishly peach beach complexion with the wrapped cotton trousers of a Thai fisherman—I heard the distress in her voice as she cried out, "Mom!"

The outlying Narita Airport is surrounded by travel-poster rice fields, but during the ride in, all I saw was my daughter's beautiful face. At the hotel we were welcomed by a fleet of uniformed greeters poised to anticipate our every imaginable need in that lobby the size of a vaulted railroad station, and though our Japanese-style room overlooked central Tokyo, we decided to postpone exploring it because there was already so much to see in the city-within-a-city of The New Otani.

First investigating its ancient classic garden in the chrysanthemum-perfect light of that October evening, as we reentered the main building we found a street-like corridor lined with a series of specialty restaurants from which to choose our first meal. Not even in what I assume to be the birthplace of Sushi would this be an option for my daughter, but you may still ask—I still ask myself—why we continued along to the corridor's far end instead of stopping for the more obvious Tempura or Teriyaki that, later in our trip, would thankfully correct for the mistake we were about to make.

Instead, we entered the *Okahan* restaurant as if Kobe beef was our destiny, and before the hot hand towels had a chance to cool, I'd ordered us the deluxe version. My limited math skills were always a liability—let's see: if JPY 3000 = $24, what's 15,750 each?—but it surprised me to find that, once we got past the entry-level greetings and the cooking pot was put before us, I didn't prove capable of retrieving any of those exceedingly polite phrases I used to know.

Once, I might have been able to explain to our server that, while in the venerable tradition of her culture such exquisitely marbled beef is a delicacy, to us—I'm sorry—*sumimasen*—it looks unappetizingly fatty. Or, with my sincerest apologies, I could have explained that it was I, certainly not her, who ought to have remembered to warn my daughter about the raw egg she was expected to drag her food through to cool it.

The larger problem was that, since it was apparently our server's job to kneel beside our table throughout the meal—*so desuka*, I said to acknowledge her "experienced chef" status, as proclaimed on the menu—it was impossible for my daughter to simply drape a boiled cabbage leaf over everything else on her plate and call it a day. All the color had drained from her face, so it wouldn't work for me to eat either. Not that I was tempted to risk it.

Across the otherwise empty restaurant, it was a relief to sense that another pair of western tourists acted like perfect guests, wildly appreciative of the colorless raw vegetables tightly arranged like wedged petals, and of course exclaiming over the white-swirled purple beef so thinly sliced, with such skilled precision, that it was almost transparent. They were eager to be taught how to scramble their raw eggs with their chopsticks, and after consuming everything on the platter, yes, they could still make room for green tea ice cream. Needless to say, they'd kept on ordering sake refills too, another failure on our part to get with the program.

In the end, our chef proved not so "experienced" as to know how to cope with such disappointed customers, but eventually she capitulated by mutely clearing away the platters and unplugging the cooker. Our folded legs were numb, and my jetlag—was it yesterday or tomorrow, back home?—exaggerated my clumsiness in factoring up the surreal calculation. In case I'd failed to take note on the menu, I was gently reminded—so now it was our uneasy chef's turn to apologize—that the total amount was "excluding service charge."

# Gnaw Thanks

## *Catherine Doty*

I've never been fussy about food, though I think I can be discerning. I have food *issues*, I'm sure...nothing dramatic or diminishing; just the need to submit the subject (and all others) to robust OCD stomping. It *is* pretty much all good (meals, I mean), if you consider what passes as a bad meal hereabouts. However, without getting all preachy here, I'm trying to figure out why I so often ruminate over the two childhood stories that follow. I don't know why, but they come together as a sort of *confuse-bouche*, in which I gently gnaw the bones of scarcity just before landing deep in the fat of campus life.

The first is about the year I entered Kindergarten. I got home each day just as my mother was serving a hot lunch to my father, who worked in a cookie factory in the next town. As he ate, he filled my mother in on the latest doings at Federal Sweets and Biscuit, and I stood behind his chair, praying loudly that he'd leave something gravyish or eggy on his plate for me. *Rhoda Robideaux's mom got a knob lopped off*, he declared, as my mother glared and pointed over his shoulder to where I knelt. Once he sputtered, *In Russia he had all the milk he wanted, and he coulda got smart off those books.* If he left something for me I'd lap it up, getting with it just a waft of his rather noisy aftershave as he rose to head back to work.

Second story: a guy my father worked with insisted we all come for dinner. He was from Alabama, and in the witty way of Federal Sweets & Biscuit, his nickname was Johnny Reb. At this dinner, in addition to *fried chicken*, his wife Suzy served me my first baking powder biscuit, the eating of which required two different kinds of jelly, right smack in the middle of the consumption of more serious supper things. I can still summon up the taste as sharply as I can the sound of my grandmother's doorbell. Not only that, but those biscuits didn't run out: they stayed on the table lounging steamily in case you wanted another nine. I had gotten into the habit of saying things I thought were funny or nice, and thought it was time to offer Suzy a lovely compliment, so I hollered, "Boy, you'd have to count to a hundred if we ever had these, right Mom?" My hosts smiled but clearly had no idea what I was talking about, so I quit talking and ripped through a few private prayers that I leave this place bearing biscuits. When we got home my mother told me that making everyone at the table over ten count to twenty before they dive onto the food isn't ritual in all families. It was her method of making sure her younger, weaker children got a head start before her teenage boys hit the table.

Like most of the families around us, sometimes we'd run out of money, make enemies, make pests of ourselves, make some odd meals. When we were beyond spaghetti and ketchup fold-overs, my dad came home with a black plastic sack on his shoulder and slammed it like moolah onto the table, but it wasn't moolah, it was cookie dough. We jumped on it with knives and carved off chunks to streak with the heels of our hands onto baking sheets and the backs of cake pans. The oven was fired up already, and in it a dozen caramel muffins were almost done. (You would never find little jars of arcane condiments or platters of leftovers in our refrigerator: my mother bought only the basics and used up every can and box— often in frightening ways—before she admitted defeat and we went the muffin-and-cookie-dough route.) We pirated the baby's milk and all had tea. I loved it.

When I finally grew into my appetite I was hitchhiking to and from Upsala College, which was twenty breezy Garden State Parkway miles from my home in Paterson. I loved every aspect of school life, and could not get over the largesse of college meals.

Though others disparaged the institutional, weighed-portion look of it, I loved the martial rows of plated desserts, each square of cake with a thumbprint in the frosting. And what was not to love about plenty and warm? I didn't care if it was stirred with a Zamboni or extruded like foam insulation; you could call it Mystery Meat or Barf-on-a-Bun. It was part of my scholarship package: let the smart kid eat.

To mask my shameful gratitude, I bitched about the food louder than anyone else. After each meal, I drew on a napkin a choking crow, from whose beaky maw flew a chunk of whatever was most disappointing: fish slabs as arid as the western states they resembled, clots of gluey au gratin potatoes. I propped my art artfully up on a dirty plate and sent it on the conveyor belt into the kitchen. Then, in the romantic, beefy, blowing-leafy twilight, waddled back to the dorm with four chocolate milks in my pockets to add to the arsenal hoarded on my windowsill.

And good luck with that hoarding thing—in those long hours between feedings, we girls were driven nuts by our bodies' need to slap on the freshman fifteen, and would steal each other blind. In the cramped and cruddy little cube of a fridge we shared, plastic containers of lasagna from home were labeled "medicine" or "I have crabs," or "don't be a bitch my grandma made it." Some fool left half an Entenmann's Ultimate Crumb Cake, from which nothing short of a layer of horn-piping maggots could dissuade me, with "I licked this" written on the box. I left the empty box with the "c" crossed out.

I do not mean that ethics never trumped greed. When the telephone company flagged several huge oak trees to be felled, we girls lashed our tie-dyed, gypsy-skirted, hash-fortified selves to their trunks and threatened to go down with them. We may, I fear, have sung or recited something druidic .I am certain that Roseanne wore frog puppets on her hands, and spent the afternoon channeling skewed statistics through her fists at anyone desperate enough to offer us their attention. Men in yellow hard hats pointed in our faces and laughed, and Lisa, retrieving some detail of a sit-in past, snarled, *How would you like your brother to come home in a box?* We were getting desperate. Tonight was Lutfisk night, and we hungered for the sight of Swedish students partaking of salt cod reconstituted with slaked lime. Still, we stood our ground, except for the few times we took turns racing into Hahne's to use the ladies' room. Hugging my tree, and holding Roseanne's frogs so she could take yet another leak, I felt noble and wild. By six we decided we'd won. The hard hat guys went past us into the bars, and we to our dining hall. As we dug into thirds of the bread pudding, the scraping of our spoons was drowned out by the screech of buzz saws.

.

# Kosher Blues

*Lisa del Rosso*

I was so goddamn hungry, I thought I was going to faint.

"Can't we stop at that deli so I can get a bit of tuna or something? There wasn't time for a late breakfast or lunch," I said, as we walked from the Baldwin train station to my sister-in-law's house.

"No, Lisa. We're going there for a Seder; there'll be a big meal and if you eat now, you'll ruin your appetite."

"You know, you're my age and you sound like my mother."

Mark made a noise I associated with one an adult makes before he reprimands a small child.

"There will be a ton of food and I'm asking you to wait. It will be rude if you don't eat the meal they spent all day preparing."

"I promise to eat the meal regardless of the doughnut I want to eat now."

"We'll be there in ten minutes. Just wait."

"Can't you break into the stuff in the shopping bag?"

"The Nut Krakowski? That's for dessert."

"Better that than the kosher wine you've got there."

"No, Lisa. I'm not opening the kosher gifts."

"But I'm hungry now!"

"You have no patience whatsoever."

"You knew that when you married me!"

"We're almost there."

"I hate you!"

"Fine," Mark said, as we walked up the front steps and rang the bell.

Everyone was already there, because we were late: Mark's brother, sister and their respective spouses, with three children per couple. My mother-in-law, Libby, greeted us, and raised her arms for a hug from Mark, not getting out of the wheelchair we all knew she did not need.

She patted his back, smiled up at him, then said, "Did you eat bread this week? I asked you not to eat bread this week! For me, you couldn't just do it for me, could you?" said Libby, her voice getting louder by the second.

"Mom... it just... it just doesn't..." Mark faltered.

Libby turned her gaze towards me. "Do you mind if he doesn't eat bread?"

I said, "I don't eat bread, so it makes no difference to me whether he does or doesn't."

Libby turned back towards Mark. "You see! Lisa doesn't mind!"

Mark shook his head back and forth. "That's not the point."

Libby wheeled her chair closer to Mark. "Your grandparents and all they went through! They'd be ashamed! ASHAMED!"

I was not inclined to get into this debate, because as far as I was concerned, they were arguing about food, I was still starving hungry and Mark hadn't bothered to feed me. So he was on his own.

"You just came here for the free meal!" Libby yelled.

I saw the sweat beginning to bead on Mark's upper lip. "Mom, I just don't believe in it. I'd be a hypocrite to not eat bread because it wouldn't mean anything to me."

Libby thrust a pointed finger up to Mark's face. "You don't believe in anything, that's your problem! You don't care about anything!"

Adjusting my watch, I thought, well, that part's not true, plus, the longer this went on, the longer I would have to wait for dinner.

"Me," I said firmly.

Libby looked over at me, and said irritably, "What are you saying?"

I said, "Me. He cares about me."

Mark, suddenly relieved, smiled and said, "That's right, Mom. I care about Lisa."

"Oh well," said Libby, "You're a pair," and she threw down her hands in disgust, as if to push us both away.

This was my first proper Seder: there had been others, but we had been so late we missed the ceremony that goes along with them. Haggadahs were passed out and read, the ritual gone through. I liked the ritual of the Seder. I liked the washing of the hands, the eating of the bitter herb, the reading aloud of a language I did not understand. It reminded me of my long-ago Catholic days: praying, sitting, standing, kneeling, eating the wafers, and making the sign of the cross. But what I remembered most about sitting in church was a gnawing hunger: my stomach would rumble in anticipation of my mother's wonderful Italian Sunday dinner, consisting of some kind of homemade pasta first, then a salad course, then a meat course, then dessert and coffee.

I was ravenous now, bordering on nausea.

For reasons unknown to me, I was seated with the young teens at end of the long dining room table. Mark was three seats down from me. I was waiting for the real meal to start, wondering what kind of food there would be. When Mark broke his fast after Yom Kippur, he brought in bagels, lox, cream cheese, and I made a salad, boiled some eggs, and added a nice goat cheese. I assumed here the food would be the same.

The first platter passed from the head of the table, where Libby sat, down towards my end, contained food I had never seen on any Italian table, nor during my married life, where I did all the cooking. There was an enormous pile of chilled chopped liver coming at me, and, after a whiff, I had no choice other than to simply pass the platter. The six teens passed also.

"You don't like chopped liver?" Libby bellowed.

"No, sorry," I said.

"What about you all, from nice Jewish families?" This she addressed to the teens, and the answers ranged from a few shrugs, to just, "No," to "Yuck." Another platter came down, containing a huge mush of whitefish salad and I passed it.

"You don't eat whitefish either, Lisa?" Libby shouted.

"No, sorry, sorry," I said.

At least I was in good company: the teens would touch nothing that looked remotely glutinous. Gefilte fish came down, and that reminded me of the green jellied eels I used to see on the stalls in the East End of London. I passed it. Libby said nothing this time, but gave me the stink eye of disgust. Christ! I thought, nothing edible! I calculated that if I fainted, I'd never get fed, so best to try and hold on. Finally, matzo ball soup came out, and my end of the table was so hungry we practically upended it to get to the steaming bowls of chicken broth that surrounded giant matzo balls. But there were a lot of people at the table, so each of us got one matzo ball and that's it.

"There's chicken coming, everyone!" said Libby.

Good, I thought, good, good, good, and not a moment too soon. The large chicken that came out for the main course was a color I had never seen on a chicken before. It was white. White, swimming in a pool of blood, with quills still sticking out of its back. I couldn't look at Libby, because there was no way I was touching it. And I could have been hallucinating, but when Mark's sister went to the kitchen to get a carving knife, I swear I heard Libby say, "I could have done better." But I'm not sure, because starvation plays tricks on the mind.

For accompaniments, a dry potato kugel may as well have been stale cereal. The iceberg lettuce, the sole ingredient of the salad, had no dressing on it. I didn't know whether to laugh, cry, or throw a knife at Mark, a man who indiscriminately ate everything and anything when he was very hungry. He had been aware of my empty plate for some time, and kept mouthing the words, "I'm sorry," in my direction. I kept mouthing back, "I hate you MORE."

We cleared off the table, I did the dishes and then made coffee while Mark brought out the dessert. When he got me alone in the kitchen, he said, "Lisa, I'm sorry, I really, really am."

Steaming, I said, "Let me tell you something, bagel man. The next time we come to one of your family gatherings, you are going to let me eat beforehand. In fact, you are going to take me out for a nice lunch, and if you don't want to eat anything, you don't have to. You can just sit there and watch me. Get it?"

"Yes, definitely yes. On behalf of all Jews, I apologize for our lack of cuisine."

"Listen, funnyman, I now know all about the lack of cuisine. I just don't want to be prevented from eating because you think I will spoil my appetite, which, by the way, I still have."

"Understood, understood. But I think I can help you right now."

I crossed my arms, and sulked. "How?"

"I think the chocolate roll will be very, very yummy."

At that, I lit up immediately, jumped up and down and said, "Let's do it!"

And we both stood in the kitchen, stuffing bits of Nut Krakowski into each other's mouths until we both were sated.

# Vile Memories

## *Walter Cummins*

Unlike my wife, I remember the worst meals I've ever had. She remembers the best. Her two favorites, really just parts of meals that she has savored with sensory vividness for years, are a bowl of consommé at a restaurant called Dirty Nelly's (founded 1620) in Bunratty, Ireland and chocolate gateaux at a small restaurant in the Denfort-Rochereau area of Paris that we wandered into one evening. It was one of those places catering to a clientele of locals who applaud every time the chef emerges from the kitchen to display his latest concoction.

What struck me was the ambience and the nodding faces as the chef leaned over each table with the plate on a white napkin. I suppose the food was good. Most French food is. For me, the meals blur. My taste buds are mundane. But I certainly know what I can't stomach.

Although I'm an anglophile, a sucker for a quaint village pub and a thatched roof, my two worst meals ever were in England. Just behind them in third and fourth place on the unpalatable scale are dishes served in that country at an institutional dining hall I eat in every January. At first glance, they were deceptive. In one case, I was expecting poached eggs that appeared to be floating in water. It was cooking oil. That may be a British favorite, like the processed peas I can't abide either. Even more of a culinary shock was the serving I took to be spaghetti and pasta sauce. The first bite puzzled me. The second told me—spaghetti with sweet and sour sauce. Perhaps the chef was hoping to emulate the creativity of that

Parisian master. Or perhaps he just opened the wrong can.

My actual second-worst meal happened in a Wimpy's close to Paddington Station and the hotel I was staying in during a solitary week in London. It was near midnight and I had walked from the theatre district on my way back from yet another play. I don't recall what play, but I do remember I was very hungry.

My friend Lisa—coincidentally—also had one of her worst meals at a Wimpy's on her very first day in London. She remembers it in gruesome detail: "It was bad beyond belief! The next meal was as bad, and made for me, and came in a stack on a plate: toast on the bottom, then on top of that, in this order, were baked bean, chips (fries), and topped off with two runny eggs sunny-side up! Gross!!" Mine was just a simple burger—flat and black on the bun, resembling a coagulated wafer of grease. What made me pick up the bun and take a bite? Probably hunger, fatigue, and automatic pilot. Grease it was. I spit out on the plate and tasted that unswallowed bite for days despite the pints of bitter I hoped would serve as an antidote.

As bad as that burger was, it still takes second place to the meal at a service area at the M4 motorway the day we drove from Kent to Cornwall. This time I had witnesses to verify my reaction—wife and two daughters. We had been on the road for several hours, all hungry, with no alternative source of food. Our expectation was just ordinariness, not the abyss.

We chose the fish plate, assuming fish and chips was a national staple, something the cook could turn out with one hand tied behind his apron. Not that cook. Not that fish. It came as a slab, the hardened grey crust slick with oil, when cracked with a fork, revealing a few shriveled bits of rancid fish flesh within. Four plates pushed back. Up and out of that restaurant as quick as we could, grabbing packets of potato crisps and candy bars to fortify us through the rest of the trip.

Don't get me wrong. I've had some decent meals in England. Edible, some even good. It's just that they can't cleanse the vile memories from my palate.

# Carving Salmon

## *Sudeep Sen*

*for Dan, Tsur & Amir*

The besotted fish —
  finless in its flight —
stares dead straight

  at Mount Zion
from the ochre stone's
  wavering opacity.

The waterless valley
  dips between
Mishkenot Sha'ananim

  and The Old City —
inviting us
  to swim despite

the unsure tide
  and times,
time that ticks

  in uneasy silence —
just like peace
  destroyed by pieces

of broken bits —
  missiles, arrows, fins,
shell bones, and fate —


*Cinematheque Restaurant,*
*Jerusalem 1997*

# The Food Wars of My Childhood

*Kenneth Smoady*

When I was a child—and I suppose there are psychological reasons for this or merely that I was so spoiled I didn't understand how good a life we had with food on the table every night—it was the exceptional meal that I approached with relish. I loved crisp green iceberg lettuce doused with vinegar (a trait my son has as well) and boiled potatoes mashed in butter, very dry overcooked meat and fishcakes, because I thought they were cakes, and most deserts. The foods I hated were many, but chief among them were stewed tomatoes, stewed stringbeans, boiled spinach, lima beans, and any kind of fish which was neither a fishcake nor swordfish, which for some reason I liked very much with lemon.

Looking back on it, I suspect that it was the name of the food that made me either like or despise it—the words spinach or stewed or lima seemed to me particularly ugly to take into my mouth while lettuce and vinegar seemed to exhude a kind of complex vitality and freshness on the tongue. During Lent when the story was recounted of the evil Roman gladiator responding to poor Jesus' plea for water —"I thirst"—by handing him up a sponge soaked in vinegar, it made my saliva run pleasantly in my mouth. I liked the word saliva, too. Most words with a 'v' pleased me.

But in the case of fish, I realize now that it was not so much a matter of the fish itself, but the fact it was served with a glass of milk. Had it been accompanied by white wine or even club soda, I

151

think I could have got it down; how can you wash down fish with milk—two foodstuffs which seem the antithesis of one another.

My parents, understandably, quickly had enough of my picky eating habits, and my father would not allow me to leave the table until I had eaten everything on my plate. I was as stubborn as he, and often would sit there until long after everyone else finished, after my mother had washed the dishes and wrapped and put away the left-overs and even reheated the food I had refused to eat, but still we were locked in a stalemate.

Then one day I tried the daring gambit, when my mother had turned her back, of scooping the stewed green beans onto the floor beneath the dining table and saying, "Mmmmm. They were delicious!"

She turned back and looked happy. "Good boy!" she exclaimed. "Wonderful!" And I was on my way up to my room, liberated, free to play with my soldiers or read until I heard her cry from the kitchen: "What is *this* under the table! Kenneth! Come down here right this instant!"

In the case of boiled spinach my mother showed some pity. She would serve me a portion that was no more than a table spoon which I would take in one mouthful and swallow whole. My three older siblings would gather round to watch this entertaining spectacle as I gagged and fought to hold the globus of bitter green rot in my esophagus long enough to swallow it.

I also devised a method to deal with my fish by taking small bites and going at once for the milk, ostensibly to wash it down, but in fact I would spit it into the milk. When the fish was all gone, I asked my mother whether I had to finish my milk. Because milk had never been a problem food for me and because she was so delighted that I had ingested the hated fish, I was excused from the milk—until my oldest brother put his nose into my affairs, saying, "I bet he spit the fish into the milk!" and held the glass up to the light. He had been joking, but was amazed to see from the gloppy residue at the base of the milk glass that that indeed was what I had done. In one second I had gone from being a good boy again to being a very bad one. I saw no moral imperatives in all of this—to me it was war, to me my task was to protect the inviolability of my body against the onslaught of hated substances.

And in the long run, I won the food wars. And I won them during the very worst meal I had ever been forced to eat: macaroni and cheese. What could be an uglier phrase than that, an uglier combination of words and letters—all those c's and e's and the succession of a-a-o-i. The mere sound of that combination of letters made me fear I would vomit, but my father was himself fed up, so to speak, with my behavior.

"You will eat that, and you will eat it now!" he shouted. I could hear he meant business, and I was overpowered, outwilled, a mere boy against the huge flannel-shirted chest and resounding male voice of a 45-year-old mustachioed and broad-jawed man.

"Eat it! Now!"

Sniffling back tears I scooped it into my mouth, forkload after forkload until my mouth was stuffed with the horrible multiple c's and double e's and all those stringy vowels of this food torture. Then, mouth filled with it, without chewing, I began to swallow, fighting back gags, grabbed for my glass to help flood it down to my stomach on a river of milk. I got it down. For a moment. Then gagging once, twice, thrice, I regurgitated it upon my plate.

"You did that on purpose!" my father bellowed. He looked around at the others. "The boy is recalcitrant" Back at me, "Eat it again!"

I was broken. There was no end to the horror of life. I was being made to eat vomit! I forked up a load of the stuff, but this was even too much for my siblings; they may have found it enormously entertaining to watch me gag on my spinach, but drew the line at agreeing to my being made to eat stuff that had already been in my stomach. My sister led the attack against the old man.

"You can't make him eat that! It's throw-up!"

My brothers joined in. My mother said nothing, but it was clear from her face that her sympathies were with me. My father looked from one face to the other, and it was clear from his face that he had been defeated.

"Ah, to hell with it!" he barked. "To hell with it all. Let him get rickets! Let him starve to death if that's what he wants!" And stomped out of the kitchen to the whiskey cabinet in his study, and I knew that I had triumphed.

From that day on, I was never forced to eat anything I did not want. A skinny little bird, I subsisted on a diet of lettuce and vinegar, peanut butter and jelly sandwiches and milk and the few other things I found palatable.

While I never developed the muscles of Popeye and never excelled at sports, neither did I ever get rickets or any other serious illness. Oddly, today there is almost no food that I do not find delicious, accompanied by a glass of wine of the appropriate color and vintage.

# The Quarter Million Dollar Chicken Filet

*Sean Finucane Toner*

West Philly traffic, potholes, a fully occupied parking garage—these should be the few remaining barriers to my finally eating that one meal, that first normal meal. Pancreas on the fritz, I've been diabetic almost from go. My every bite has been counterbalanced against calculated doses of injected insulin, every gram of sugar prodded with needles.

But only a little longer. My uncle Bob and I are heading to HUP—the Hospital of the University of Pennsylvania—to drop by the transplant ward for a few part replacements. I'm aware of the gravity of the event, but I liken the operation to pulling in for car repairs. Only a year ago the kidneys blew out too, and now I have to count every drop of water in every glass and every grain of rice, as well. My blood isn't purified normally and it has to be filtered at a dialysis center three times a week before I drown in diet soda or am poisoned by the potassium in my mashed potatoes. But I'll no longer have to fear death by tuber once I get my new filter change at Jiffy Kidney.

Sports radio plays in the car. Football. Talk of some injury or trade elicits more concern from Bob, and this is the way it should be. Though I'm nearing thirty, and he's in his fifties, there's a kind of jocular frat-boy relationship between us that's kept me sane through my medical troubles. "This doesn't look good," he says when we near the hospital.

Donor organs don't last long in coolers, and I'm hearing the tic-tic-tic of individual grains of sand hitting the pile in the egg timer.

"I don't think this is a street," Bob adds. He backs out of the paved walk and is all "I'm sorry," and "excuse me," and "my mistake." But his voice is at conversational level. It's for my benefit—not for the pedestrians in the area. He's fulfilling his obligation to be cavalier.

Once parked, we're through the hospital labyrinth. Skybridge, lobby, corridor after corridor until I'm certain we're about to encounter bones or sleeping minotaur. We meet my girlfriend Melody at admissions.

Later—too much later—I'm on the gurney, I.V. in, readying to have what has failed in me replaced by what is left of a generous other. Melody kisses me. Bob has his own way. "Better you than me," he says, one of our shared catch phrases.

"First hundred years are the toughest," I throw back.

He pats my arm and I'm wheeled in. There's bustle about the room as my I.D. bracelets are checked, as the operating lamp is adjusted, as packages are opened and surgical instruments are laid out on the stainless steel cart.

The anesthesiologist places the breathing tubes in my nostrils, tells me he's about to inject me through my I.V. "You'll be out in less than ten seconds."

I count—not too quickly—to fourteen. I must show I'm more than mechanized flesh, more than a clockwork orange.

Good news, though, is that when it's all done, I'll finally be allowed to dine with the most seductive dinner companion: impunity.

§

Without functioning kidneys, it's been like a bus trip sans working bathroom, sans pullovers. Now, several days post-transplant, I stand with feet on cold floor and pee for the first time in a year. I sway a little, want to adjust aim and fancy myself spelling out my name on a winter snow.

"Woo-hoo!"

Running the tap, my first labor, is done. Two more tasks and I'm a free man.

The second item—making sure the other pipes have not been damaged during the surgery—does not come so easily. Nurses and assistants are through the door all day and night taking temperatures, weighing me, measuring output, sending the antirejection pills through the tube in my nose—first—and then the old-fashioned way nature meant us to swallow steroids and cyclosporine. At breaks of day, phlebotomist Angela, with her Caribbean accent, draws blood. Doctors, of course, en masse during the morning rounds, then one specialty at a time throughout the day: endocrinologists, nephrologists, a urologist. All this so that I can order a Happy Meal without drawing on my prep-school calculus.

There's little chance for rest, and hospitals are no haven for the unwell. The procession continues, ceaseless, the snake Ouroboros consuming its tail: cleaning people, itinerant ministers and the food service woman with her taunts of "Are you ready for a menu, yet?"

My grandmother (please God, no more political talk) and her mortician sister (please God, no pocketed tape measure) pay daily visits. My mom's in, a little shaky, and she's convinced the transplant has transformed me in a mystical way.

"Do you smell fire?" I ask one day.

"This whole place is non-smoking," she says, dejected.

"Sure you don't smell fire?" I insist.

Later, she reports that there has been a fire at the Philadelphia Art Museum at the same time I kept asking. "You've had a psychic awakening," she says.

Bob and wife Lynn are in, a random number of my five cousins, Granny's priest friends eager to hear confession. A nun or two, and of course, Melody braving it through my health issues while she suffers from (as yet undiagnosed) lupus.

Phone calls. Everybody. My dad, sis Christi, ex-girlfriends, neighbors, and a wrong number for someone on the cardiac floor.

And Zonk.

Bob plays switchboard operator at home, says, "All right, I've got the phone to his ear."

And I'm "Hey Zonk. How are you dude?" I keep that up for a few until I'm beginning to feel a bit silly.

"I don't know what you were telling him," Bob says when he's back on, "but he was sniffing the earpiece." It's as close to a "get well soon" as I'm going to receive from the striped tabby.

Once I finally get that second task, dropping a deuce, done, a nurse has to check for blood in my stool.

"How does it look?" I ask.

"It's green" she says.

"Where'd you get my organs, area 51?"

Though there's a rising white count troubling the doctors, I'm finally cleared to fill out a menu. It may have been Mom, could have been Mel, probably nurse Randi who ran through it with me. We speed through the next day's meal choices and we light on dinner. "Roast chicken breast?"

"Sounds good."

"Or beef stew?"

"Don't mind if I do."

But I don't. When breakfast comes, I don't advance too far. It's shrunken stomach after weeks of not eating, I think. The food isn't that great—that must be it. At lunchtime, I only have a desire for the mashed potatoes. When dinner comes, it smells appetizing. I am eager to prove the new organs worthy, but cautiously begin with the dessert cake. Then the applesauce. Sweets seem the smoothest road out of nausea. But when I start with the stew, I'm in for only a few bites before everything I've taken in decides it wants back out.

"Didn't like your food?" the staff person in charge of trays asks when she returns.

"I've had worse."

The food service woman takes my tray away. A watery mess of consumed food, the most recently imbibed liquids, napkins, and a sense of security with my new organs exit the room. Something isn't working.

§

Biopsies, laparoscopies and blood tests all lead to one ugly conversation. We have to off the pancreas before it offs me. A profound disappointment, yes, and it's to be a seventh surgery in a year. But I am not alarmed until an unknown priest knocks, offers a serving of Last Rites. "Just in case," he says.

I'm not all that churchy, but I let him stamp my sacramental passport. Just in case.

The kidney remains kicking, the surgery goes smoothly but then my adventure takes an odd little turn. I wander off into a week-long hallucination involving shopping malls, beergartens, a winded Japanese angel, and me as a gurney-bound flying target at a driving range. There's also a surfer-dude demon with a seven-barreled pistol that looks more like a syrinx. The remote with the button for the morphine drip is taken from my hand.

A week after the pancreas removal—nearly a month since I was first admitted—I awake to learn I've been moved to a room in front of the nurse's station. "Remind me which are the cute ones," I ask Bob, and all concerned are not so worried anymore.

I seem to be regaining my appetite.

The nephrologist, the endocrinoligist, a cardiologist, the transplant chief and a new guy—a psychiatrist—all okay me to eat. Same band of cooks plus one.

I brazenly go with the chicken filet, rice and Jell-o for my first lunch. These last two items are plump with water I would have had to weigh a month ago. I down the meal with my then-preference, diet Dr. Pepper. It's champagne brought from home.

The chicken filet and the rice ache for salt, and the hospital seasoning packets just don't cut it for me. But I eat. And it is good. In a relative sort of way. The way fast food burgers are great—for a buck.

Once I demonstrate that my new kidney is still fully functioning I'm a free man. I'm released to the Tonerarium, my extended-family home. One noon, I pass Zonk, sphinx-like on the stool by the fridge, but he's really Pharaoh as he wills us to serve him. I pull open a can and drink to my heart's content. At lunch, I'm metabolicly back to the way I'd been most of my life. And Zonk is on the table, lending an assist to my smoked turkey sandwich, pawing at the schnibbles I put on the plate for him.

Mail arrives during lunch, and this day the statement from the hospital comes in a thick manila envelope. The six weeks are described in painful detail. The last dialysis treatment, the transplant, the laparoscopy, the MRIs and the CAT scans, the untransplant. The documents are ripe with numerals culminating with a reserved "Wow" from Lynn.

"How much?" I ask.

"This can't be right," she says. Medicare and Blue Cross have covered all but the incidentals like TV and phone. But the damage is just shy of $250,000. And how much of a tip do you leave after a meal like that?

And to whom?

# Portuguese Garden Buffet

*Thomas E. Kennedy*

You are attending a welcome buffet for an international conference in the gardens of a lavish mansion in sunny Oporto. You have dreamed of visiting Portugal since that day, as a lad, you fell in love with Piper Laurie in *Beneath the Twelve Mile Reef*, about sponge-diving in this country. Now you are here with a group of young professionals that includes an Icelandic woman who looks nothing like Piper Laurie other than that she is just as piping hot. You flirt a bit with her. She flirts back a bit. The sun is high in the clear blue vault of the sky. Life is good.

The buffet includes all manner of delicacy sparkling in the sunlight, and you stand over the sumptuous array, trying to decide where to begin: The baby eels white and worm-like squirmed alluringly together in a yellow sea of garlic olive oil? The boiled eggs, halved and stuffed with a curry-colored mayonnaise dressing? The tiny boiled shrimp with lemon and dill? The grilled tiger shrimp with lime and dill? Perhaps you should start with a delectable portion of fingers of Icelandic beauty? Nibble nibble yum.

The host, Pedro, a jovial dark fellow shorter than yourself and with protruding teeth that make his smile even more jovial, steps up to you. He seems to think you speak French. "Tomas," he exclaims. "Mon ami! My best friend in Europe! Ca va?"

"Ca va," you respond.

"Eat!" he orders. "You like thee baby eels?"

You tell him you love eels, though you have never tasted baby ones, and spoon a squirming nest of them onto your plate alongside the tiny shrimp, the tiger shrimp, and several deviled eggs. Out of the corner of your eye, you notice that the Icelandic girl is now flirting with a German fellow. Perhaps she flirts with everybody. No matter. Focusing your appetite upon organs of gestation, you scoop an entire halved deviled egg into your mouth and munch happily. How delightfully it fills your gob, yielding delicately to your palate which you clear with a crisply crusted nugget of Portuguese barley bread. The utensils are of silver. Upon the Sterling tines, you impale several tiny white eels, dripping with garlic-savory oil and fork them into your mouth.

O brave new world that has such creatures in it! And then, because fish must swim, you chase the little things with a stream of chilled, exquisitely dry white port. How wonderful to chew and drink at one and the same time, violating all rules of childhood. Now tiny boiled shrimp are on the tines, now in your mouth, and they of course also must swim; now grilled tigers that swim as well, though requiring a stronger current. And now another egg—with curry and chili and olive—more bread to munch, and another pitchfork full of baby eel, not caring that they hang like catfish whiskers through your lips. There is no happiness like yours! You have been eating baby eels!

The sun caresses the flesh of your short-sleeve-shirted arms, touches your forehead with tender warmth. You squint through the delightful light at the Icelandic girl who having flirted, by turn, with an Italian and a Finn, comes back to flirt a bit more with you. It occurs to you that she is a female juggler of male hearts, honing her ability to keep—so to speak— many balls in the air. No matter. Batter my heart, Icelandic girl! Lest you rape me, I will not be chaste!

Pedro is back now, too. "You my best friend in Europe, Tomas! Ca va?"

"Ca va, Pedro." This is wonderful.

The Icelandic girl turns her ice-blue eyes upon brown Pedro. His protruding teeth flash at her. Pedro's face seems to be rippling before your eyes. It occurs to you that you are feeling a bit tipsy. Or perhaps it is the sun.

But several hours later, you will learn it is neither the wine nor the sun. You will learn this while trapped inside the closet-sized hotel elevator with the Icelandic girl—which would be fine except that there are half a dozen young international professional men in that closet-sized car with you as well: A Swede, a Norwegian, an Italian, Frenchman, German, you and the Icelandic girl who, after the stalled elevator has not moved for five full minutes of boiling heat, says, "I am feeling not so well."

You chuckle. Good joke! But then you look into her ice-blue eyes and see there clouds of northern terror. There is a moment of intense silence. Is the Icelandic girl going to throw up? Regardless which direction she does it in, someone—several—will be splashed. You do not wish her to throw up on you. You exchange glances with the others in the elevator; all eyes have a similar fixation of terror.

And then you hear the bubbling.

Chancing what you hope might be the relief of humor, you ask, "Is that mine stomach or thine?"

The Swede says, "I think it is a fucking full chorus!"

A harmony of bubbling stomachs. In minor key. You feel like stout Cortez upon a peak in Darien gazing down into the chemic broil of non-pacific waves. You feel you are on a boat. Your head is swimming. Your brain is full of baby eels!

At just that moment a voice comes from above, as if the voice of God: "The elevator is stuck," pronounces the voice. "Are you all all right?"

"I do not know to whom you are addressing," says the Icelandic girl, "but I am not all right. Not!"

"We are going to have to hand crank the elevator," says the voice. "Bon courage!"

The elevator begins very slowly to descend in time with the screeching sound of what could only be the hand crank, which sounds rather rusty.

"He wasn't fucking kidding!" says the Swede just as the car jolts to a stop, and the voice from above says, "Oops!"

"What the fuck do you mean by Oops?" demands the Swede—his exclamation is followed by a chorus of baritone laughter that does not sound particularly happy.

"We missed the floor," says the voice. "It is difficult to stop with the hand crank. We shall have to crank you all the way down to the basement. Hold tight. It might be a rough ride."

And that is when the first passing of gas becomes discernible. It seems to hit all nostrils at once, but it is the Swede who puts words to this new aspect of our collective agony.

"What the fuck?!" he exclaims. "Who the fuck did that?!"

Half a dozen male voices sing out in unison, "Wasn't me!" If we are all telling the truth, this means that the Icelandic beauty is the author of this very foul emission. You chance a glance, and the flaming red of her blush tells all.

"I lied," you say then. "It was I. Scuse me." This is not a ploy to score cheap points. It is the curse of having been raised Irish Catholic. You know how guilty of everything you are any way, so you invite suffering and shame down upon your head.

The creaking of the hand crank does not completely muffle the bubbling of the bellies all around you as neither does the jolting of the stuffed elevator car assist in the tightening of buttocks. Soon someone has authored a rhyme for the Icelandic emission. Then another. Soon there is something that seems like a soup of odor rising dangerously within the little compartment.

"Oh fuck!" exclaims the Swede.

"We are going to drown in farts! "

You notice the red-bearded Norwegian make what appears to be an open-mouthed stand against gagging, but your own difficulty is with the opposite end of your alimentation. Being a literary fellow, you are remembering the early scene in Mailer's *The Naked and the Dead* in which the soldiers on the beachhead exchange the buzz phrase Keep a tight azzhole, and it occurs to you that 'fuck' was not the only word that Mailer was unable to spell.

The elevator car is jolting in a manner that makes you fear you are about to experience extreme public disgrace, but finally the car jolts a final time, and the door slides open as the voice of God pronounces you free. Seven people bolt for the stairwell—if the verb bolt can be applied to a group of human beings hobbling like ducks, a shoulder-bumping clot of humans ascending.

Your room is on the seventh floor, and you have the misfortune on the sixth floor landing to picture one of the slender white baby eels dripping with oil.

"Oh, no!" you shout.

The Swede, behind you, says, "I fuckin' know just what you mean!"

Who wrote the poem that begins after the first death there is no other? After the first public shame, there is no other either. Now instead of hobbling you are hopping toward the door of your room, dancing a tarantella as you insert the key, and at last you stand above the glowing white commode, wondering whether to sit upon or stand over it, thinking about the agony of antagonism between this set of verbs and prepositions.

But there is no greater shame or pain for you now, you are gone, totally, abandoned to the demands of your body, and you take turns with these words, sitting over and standing on, and hugging the porcelain.

Finally, utterly depleted, wrapped in shameful odors, you limp to your bed and collapse backwards onto it. Your eyelids close. Weakly you lift them again and see before you the face of a black dog against a blood red sky.

Ah, you think. This then is how death appears, with the face of a dark hound, as you slip away into an oblivion that can only be the termination of your life upon this earth.

Some hours, perhaps days later, however, your lids lift again, and your eyeballs are staring into the face of Pedro. His lips crawl back from the protrusion of his teeth, and he asks, "Ca va?"

You say what you think is "Ca va."

"You my best friend in Europe, Tomas! We were worried about you. You have been deeply asleep for a long time."

You say, "Uhn?"

"Ever-ee bodee is sick," he tells you. "But I have investigated and learned what has happened."

"Uhn? "

He nods, smiling with the understanding of a man who knows the world and its devious ways. "The caterers," he says, "knew full well that the food was infected. They admitted this to me. And then, to kill the bacteriums, they sprayed it with insecticide. Can you believe this?"

"Uhn."

"But I have, how you say? Feexed their wagon. You know what I have done? "

"Uhn? "

"I have refused to pay them!"

# Stepping Over the Velvet Rope

*Michael Lee*

*"I went to a restaurant that serves 'breakfast at any time,' so I ordered French toast during the Renaissance."—Steven Wright*

There's a brass ring notion among would be writers and hope-to-be restaurateurs, that either trade is easy to go into and come out with some fast cash. Evidently both jobs look so elementary that a llama could do it. As a writer and former cook, I'd ask when's the last time you read a great mystery from a llama, or enjoyed a superb omelet de llama? Be careful when that brass ring looks so attainable.

I've worked in kitchens from Cape Cod to Key West, frequently sober, but with absolutely no formal training. I've also worked on a septic pumping truck in Miami which didn't require any formal training either. And so, I feel I can say with some authority, that I've seen both ends of the restaurant business.

Having worked (and eaten) in areas devoted to tourism, it appears obvious to me that the mood of customers are dependent on such variables as: sunsets, traffic, other people's sticky children, warm water in summer, snow in winter, and rapidly moving lines at miniature golf courses. You can also tell if you're eating in a tourist zone because odds are there will be pictures illustrating the menu choices. This is because most tourists leave half their brain cells at home. It is far easier to point at a lobster and say, "Ungh," than it is to try to verbalize your choice. This is especially true if you go to foreign destinations such as Massachusetts or Louisiana, where the locals speak a different language under the guise of English.

On Cape Cod in particular, finding local workers is almost impossible, so restaurants have turned to a number of foreign countries to help fill their staff. Don't be surprised if the person taking your order at an Italian restaurant is Haitian and speaks only a fractured French. This past summer the country du jour was Bulgaria and I'm still trying to figure out how I got poached salmon when I thought I pantomimed quite well for a cheeseburger and a scattering of fries.

Here's a great inside tip that will enable you to receive optimum service and friendliness no matter how wretched the food is. As you are seated at a table, immediately take out a small notebook and pen, scribbling a few incoherent lines on the first page. Lay the pen across what you've written and wait for your waitron to come get your order (waitron is less gender-specific than waiter or waitress and shows that you are way politically correct). This rule does not apply in Provincetown or Key West, where it just doesn't matter a hell of a lot and gender-hedging is de rigueur.

When your waitron approaches the table, take a look around as if you are surveying the décor. This will only reinforce that you are indeed a restaurant critic and soaking up the ambiance. It will almost always guarantee you better service, the best food possible (no matter how mediocre the talent in the kitchen) and—here's the downside—an inevitable visit to your table by the owner or maitre de, who will pretend he's always this cheery and visits every table.

There are a few other tricks of the trade you might look for. For instance, the higher the food is arranged, the more it costs. I've received teetering towers of chicken and beef surrounded by a moat of gravy. As soon as the fork enters the foray, the tower collapses, and you pluck out what doesn't float and looks edible. It still tastes like chicken and beef, but when the check arrives it invariably costs more than my first car.

You can take this observation to the bank: the more attractive the waitrons, the worse the service and food. One of the more popular seafood restaurants on Cape Cod had dreadful food all one summer because they chose to hire several women from the University of Connecticut gymnastic team and dress them in short shorts. Aside from being limber, none of the women seemed to mind the inevitable wedgies that dug in while they struggled over a heavy tray of fried clams and mussels. It was sort of a Hooters concept, only with a nod toward the lower anatomic aficionados. The place should have been called "Booters."

As for my own personal gastronomic disasters, I've had many. But easily the one that wears the crown is the time I was served a lobster that hadn't been near boiling water or a frying pan in its entire crustaceous life. I swear by all that's salty, this thing was as lively and fresh as if it had just been plucked from behind a wad of kelp or under a rock. Credit here goes to the dumbest waitron I've ever encountered—or does it? Consider the number of hands and eyes this au natural dish had to pass muster in order to arrive, squiggling and writhing, at our table. There's the so-called chef (most likely a Rumanian hot dog vendor in his native life), then there's the garnish dude, who must have attended the Jose Feliciano School of Garnishing. We can't leave out the cook who is supposed to coordinate the entire entrée and give his final blessing to it. That's before we get to the UConn waitron. Did I forget to mention our server that evening was the gymnast whose specialty was the parallel bars? I'm not sure if that has any more meaning than a waitron who excels on the balance beam, but I thought I'd throw it out there for any conspiracy enthusiasts.

I was fascinated by the life still surging through my entree, but much to my wife's horror, Lucky the Lobster was making considerable progress in its surge for freedom. It had now left my plate and was headed toward the bread basket, perhaps mistaking it for a lobster trap. Evidently, Lucky was no Rhodes Lobster. It was time for me to leap into action. Lucky was somewhat groggy and evidently missed its ration of salt water, so it was easy to grab it—even though it didn't have pegs jammed into its claws, without risking my concert piano career. Fortunately, my wife had one of those beach bags that can house a Volkswagen and in perhaps the niftiest, if not most heroic move of my dining career, I crammed the lobster in there.

"What about my god damned makeup?" she asked me. I got a glimpse of the hero's life then: lonely, misunderstood, unappreciated and underfed.

The UConn waitron stopped by eventually (maybe I should mention we ate there a couple times a week. My wife kept asking why since the food stunk. "Ah, the kids need money for school," I said, philanthropically).

She deposited the bill on our table, clearing away the plates as she did. "Wow, Mister," she said to me, "You really liked your lobster. It's like totally gone." That cleared up any mystery of whether she was on an academic or athletic scholarship. It was also the first time I can recall being called "Mister,"which made me feel as though I was in a 1930's movie with the Dead End Kids.

As for my experiences in the kitchen, I seem to have withdrawn most of the 1970's from my memory bank. I know I went through it because I still have some of the bad clothing. What few highlights I can remember, usually involved waitresses (there, I've made the distinction only to imply my hard-earned heterosexuality. I even married one of our waitresses once).

And, of course, the other factor in restaurant experience is drinking. Rather than looking for the brass ring, sex and booze are far more reliable goals. The owner of the last restaurant where I worked had heard I could run the line like Henry Ford and churn out dinners like a machine. I'd never earn a Michelin Star, hell, I didn't even use their tires, but for some reason I could run a line of meal tickets and kitchen personnel as though I was an air traffic controller. This talent for kitchen organization was purely a gift from a God with a broad sense of humor because my life on the outside is generally in turmoil. But the owner's big and costly mistake was a policy of "unlimited free drinks for the kitchen." We had 12 different entrees on the menu and 7 appetizers and I could grind those out in my sleep or my stupor. Most nights in the summer we would do 400 dinners with a three man line. And I swear I didn't know a roux from a ratatouille.

We had a very sophisticated system to call the waitrons into the kitchen to pick up their orders—I would bellow out their names, "Lisa! Kathy! Brenda!" If two or three minutes passed, I would holler louder. It worked for us. And you always wanted to make sure the waitrons picked up the correct order because we would frequently have at least two orders for separate tables assembled for pickup.

The way our tickets holder was designed and the serving table where the cooks lined up the dinners, gave us a very limited view of the waitrons. You had to make sure they got the right stuff because when you're in the middle of pumping out dinner after dinner, it can get panicky and waitrons have been known to mistake steak for shrimp, salad for desert. And raw lobster from cooked. Since only a very small portion of the waitrons were visible to the cooks, during the dinner rush we got to know each of them only by what we could see—from their belt line to the tops of their thighs. It might not be perfect science and I'm sure other restaurants have infinitely more refined systems, but it only took a week or so until I recognized everyone from their, well, specific parts. For instance, no one was as bow-legged as Brenda, and Lisa had a rear end that would stop traffic. It might sound sexist, but after all, it was how I met my first wife.

In closing, I'd like to give a warning to those readers with queasy stomachs. This final anecdote is absolutely true and utterly disgusting. By far the worst post-meal reaction I've seen occurred at a popular pub on the Cape. Monday nights were prime rib night and attracted both locals and tourists, so there was always a line waiting to get in. There was a bench outside the restaurant for smokers (in Massachusetts you practically have to get a boat and go three miles out to fire up your Marlboro) and I was hanging around talking to some of the locals. Soon a head emerged from the door and then the rest of the body lurched after it. He was one of the real regulars, a guy who already had a bar chair named after him (you usually had to die to get that honor). Let's call him Al because it's shorter to type and he might sue me if I gave his real name.

A few of us yelled, "Hey Al," to which Al tried to answer "Hi guys," but what came out was hardly a greeting. There, in front of the line of customers and his buddies on the smoke bench, Al gacked a beauty right at the front door. When he ralphed, it sounded like the voice of Erebus, condemning a poor soul in a deep tonality and looked like someone had taken a "pizza-with-the-works" and dropped it on the front step to the pub. The line responded with an audible, "Argh," half of them leaving instantly. The rest backed off considerably so there was no chance their olfactory systems were compromised. Those with strong stomachs, laughed their asses off, the rest of us gagged and headed for our cars.

I have to give some of those tourists all the credit in the world. One couple hopped over Al's visual restaurant review and went inside—I guess the prime rib looked good whether it was used or not. I know some Cadillacs do. A few more hung around, hoping the lowest person on the restaurant ladder would come out soon and make everything new again. Al, now the color of ancient plaster, said, "Whoa," and continued on down the street. For my money he was headed to the next bar, but it made him a legend among his friends. And cut way down on his dinner invitations.

And that, my friends, is the best of my worst on both sides of the velvet rope.

Bon appétit!

# About the Editors

Walter Cummins and Thomas E. Kennedy are the founders of Serving House Books.

# Contributors

RENÉE ASHLEY is the author of four volumes of poetry--*Salt* (Brittingham Prize in Poetry, University of Wisconsin Press), *The Various Reasons of Light*, *The Revisionist's Dream*, and *Basic Heart* (X. J. Kennedy Prize, Texas Review Press)--as well as two chapbooks, *The Museum of Lost Wings* and *The Verbs of Desiring*, and a novel, *Someplace Like This*. She has been awarded fellowships from the National Endowment for the Arts and the New Jersey State Council on the Arts, and is on the core faculty of Fairleigh Dickinson University's low-residency MFA Program in Creative Writing.

DUFF BRENNA is the recipient of an NEA Fellowship, and won the AWP's Best Novel award for his first novel, *The Book of Mamie*. His third novel, *Too Cool*, was a New York Times Noteworthy Book. His fourth novel, *The Altar of the Body*, was Book Editor's Favorite Book of the Year at South Florida Sun-Sentinel. Brenna's stories, poems and essays have appeared in *Cream City Review, SQ Agni, The Nebraska Review, The Literary Review, The Madison Review, New Letters* ,and numerous other literary venues. (Web: www.duffbrenna.com)

WALTER CUMMINS' fourth short story collection, *The End of the Circle*, was published by Egress Books in 2009. In addition to publishing more than 100 stories, he edited *The Literary Review* for twenty years. (Web: www.waltercummins.com)

STEVE DAVENPORT is the author of *Uncontainable Noise* (poems) and a couple of chapbooks. Recent publications include a story and a poem in *The Southern Review*, a lyrical essay in *Northwest Review* (reprinted at www.perigee-art.com), and a scholarly essay about Richard Hugo's poetry in *All Our Stories Are Here: Critical Perspectives on Montana Literature* (University of Nebraska Press).

LISA del ROSSO originally trained as a singer, and completed a post-graduate program at LAMDA (London Academy of Music and Dramatic Art), living in London and working as a performer for nine years before moving to New York City. Her play, *Clare's Room*, was performed at the 2006 New York International Fringe Festival. Her writing has appeared in a variety of publications, including *Young Minds Magazine, Time Out New York, The Neue Rundschau,* and *Writers On The Job* (http://writersonthejob.webdelsol.com/sounds. html). She reviews plays for theateronline.com, and is currently finishing a novel. Lisa was invited for a residency at the Ledig House Writer's Colony and worked as a researcher and reader for the German publishing house, S. Fischer Verlag. She received her MFA in Creative Writing from Fairleigh Dickinson University and teaches writing at NYU.

MARTIN DONOFF, the Director of the MFA in Creative Writing Program at Fairleigh Dickinson University, teaches dramatic writing and film studies. He is the author and/or story editor of more than 125 network television scripts and plays including *Alf* (NBC), *Timeline* (PBS), and *Captain Kangaroo* (CBS). He taught script writing and film studies at Drexel University where he founded the Dramatic Writing Program.

CATHERINE DOTY is the author of *Momentum*, a volume of poems from CavanKerry Press, and *Just Kidding*, a collection of cartoons published by Avocet Press. Her work has appeared in numerous magazines and anthologies, among them Garrison Keillor's *More Good Poems for Hard Times* and Billy Collins' *180 More: Extraordinary Poems for Every Day*. She is the recipient of a Marjorie J. Wilson Award, an Academy of American Poets Prize, fellowships from the New Jersey State Council on the Arts and the New York Foundation for the Arts, and other grants and honors. Ms. Doty has worked as a visiting artist for the Frost Place, the Geraldine R. Dodge Foundation, the New York Public Library, and other organizations.

THOMAS E. KENNEDY's 26 books include the four novels of *The Copenhagen Quartet*, the first of which was published world-wide by Bloomsbury USA and UK in 2010—*In the Company of Angels*. In 2010, New American Press also published his "novel in essays" *Last Night My Bed a Boat of Whiskey Going Down*. Another Copenhagen novel, *Falling Sideways*, will appear from Bloomsbury in 2011. (Web: www.thomasekennedy.com)

TERRENCE KERRIGAN is the pseudonym of a flaneur who writes regularly about the bars and bookstores of various European cities. He was himself the subject of a novel disguised as a guide to Danish and Irish serving houses, *Kerrigan's Copenhagen*, published in 2002 by Thomas E. Kennedy.

DENNYS KHOMATE, a French-American, hails from Astoria, New York. In his thirties he relocated to Europe where he has lived for some years. He has published stories and essays in various American literary journals and has worked as a speechwriter for a number of nongovernmental organizations in Dublin, Paris, Geneva, Stockholm, Helsinki, Oslo and Copenhagen.

MICHAEL LEE is a Cape Codder who served for seven years as literary editor for the biweekly newsmagazine, *The Cape Cod Voice*. His numerous short stories and articles appear in such publications as *The Yale Review, New Letters*, and *The Boston Globe Sunday Magazine*. A short story from Lee's collection, *Paradise Dance* (Leapfrog Press, 2002), won an honorable mention for a Pushcart Prize. His collection of humor essays, *In an Elevator with Brigitte Bardot*, was published by Wordcraft of Oregon in 2007. Lee is a member of PEN International, the Author's Guild, the Norman Mailer Society, and the National Book Critics Circle. He is currently working on two novels, *Dancing Man*, and a novel based on his return to Khe Sanh, Vietnam, where he wrote dispatches for *Stars and Stripes* while serving in the U.S. Marine Corps.

ALEXANDRA MARSHALL has published five novels, *Gus in Bronze, Tender Offer, The Brass Bed, Something Borrowed*, and *The Court of Common Pleas*, and a nonfiction book, *Still Waters*. Her short fiction and essays have appeared in *Agni, Five Points, Hunger Mountain, Ploughshares, The American Prospect, The Boston Globe, The Cape Cod Voice*, and *The New York Times*. She co-founded and directed The Ploughshares International Fiction Writing Seminar in Kasteel Well, The Netherlands.

THOMAS McCARTHY was born in Mallow, Co. Cork Ireland and educated there and in Dublin. He has lived in France and Ireland and now lives in Peterborough, UK His stories have been published in *PEN New Fiction 1 & 2; Sunk Island Review; Paris Transcontinental; The Literary Review; Cimarron Review; New Irish Writing; The Irish Press; StoryQuarterly*. A collection of stories, *The Last Survivor*, was published in 1985. Citron Press published a novel, *A Fine Country*, in May 2000. A further collection of stories, *Finals Day & Other Stories*, was published in October 2002. His essay "At Least You'll Never Starve" is in the collection *Writers on the Job*, published by Hopewell

Publications in the USA in 2008. His novel *The Coast of Death* will be published by Serving House Books in 2010. At present, he is at work on another novel, *Flannery's World*, and a trilogy of linked stories called *Morning Has Broken*.

RICK MULKEY is the author of four collections including *Toward Any Darkness* and *Before the Age of Reason*. Individual poems and essays have appeared in a variety of venues such as *Crab Orchard Review, Denver Quarterly, The Literary Review, The Connecticut Review, Poet Lore, Poetry East, Shenandoah*, and *Southern Poetry Review*. He currently directs the low-residency MFA in creative writing at Converse College.

VICTOR RANGEL-RIBEIRO was born in Goa in 1925 when that part of India was still a Portuguese colony. Having migrated to Bombay at the age of 13, he then began writing under a second colonial flag. Long settled in the United States, he is one of the few bi-pre-postcolonial writers to be still putting pen to paper, fingers to the keyboard, ear to the wheel, etc. Or one of the few pre-post-bicolonial writers—oh, gosh darn it, never mind.

R.A. RYCRAFT has published stories, essays, reviews, and interviews in a number of journals and anthologies, including *PIF Magazine, VerbSap, Perigee, The MacGuffin,* and *Calyx*. Winner of an Eric Hoffer Best New Writing Editor's Choice Award for 2008 and a Special Mention for the 2010 Pushcart Prize, Rycraft is chair of the English department at Mt. San Jacinto College in Menifee, California.

MIMI SCHWARTZ is the author of five books, most recently, *Good Neighbors, Bad Times, Echoes of My Father's German Village*, a winner of the ForeWord Book of the Year Award in Memoir for 2008 and of the New Hampshire Outstanding Literary Nonfiction Award. Other recent books include *Thoughts from a Queen-sized Bed*, voted a 2002 book club favorite by JCC book clubs, and *Writing True, the Art and Craft of Creative Nonfiction* (with Sondra Perl), used in writing programs nationwide. Her short work has appeared in the *New York Times, Creative Nonfiction, Agni, Missouri Review, Jewish Week, Christian Science Monitor*, and the *Writer's Chronicle*, among others. Six essays have been Notables in *Best American Essays* and two have been Pushcart Prize finalists. A veteran teacher and lecturer, Schwartz is Professor Emerita at Richard Stockton College and lives in Princeton, New Jersey.

PETER SELGIN's *Drowning Lessons* (stories, UGA Press, 2008), won the 2007 Flannery O'Connor Award for Fiction. His novel, *Life Goes to the Movies* (Dzanc Books, April 2009) was named a Best Book of the Year by *ForeWord Magazine*. His stories and essays have appeared in dozens of publications, including *Salon, The Sun,* and*Best American Essays 2006*. He is also the author of two books on writing craft, *By Cunning & Craft* and *179 Ways to Save a Novel: Matters of Vital Concern to Fiction Writers. Confessions of a Left-Handed Man,* an essay collection, is forthcoming from University of Iowa Press/Sightline Books. He edits *Alimentum: The Literature of Food*. (Web: www. peterselgin.com)

SUDEEP SEN's many books include: *Postmarked India: New & Selected Poems* (HarperCollins), *Distracted Geographies, Rain, Aria* (A K Ramanujan Translation Award), *Blue Nude: Poems & Translations 1977-2012* (forthcoming, Jorge Zalamea Poetry Award), and *The HarperCollins Book of New English Poetry by Indians* (editor).His writings have appeared in the *TLS, Guardian, Observer, Independent, London Magazine, The Literary Review, Harvard Review, Telegraph, Hindu, Outlook, India Today*, and broadcast on BBC, CNN-IBN, NDTV & AIR. Sen's recent work appears in *New Writing 15* (Granta) and *Language for a New Century* (Norton). He was international writer-in-residence at the Scottish Poetry Library (Edinburgh) and visiting scholar at Harvard University. Sen is the editorial director of AARK ARTS and editor of *Atlas* (www.atlasaarkarts.net).

KENNETH SMOADY has worked variously as a plongeur and teacher of English as a second language. He has been writing fiction, essays and poetry for many years. This is his first published work.

GLADYS SWAN has published two novels, *Carnival for the Gods* (Vintage Contemporaries Series) and *Ghost Dance: A Play of Voices*, nominated by LSU Press for the Pen/Faulkner Award. She has published six collections of short fiction, the most recent being *A Garden Amid Fires*. Her short fiction has appeared in such literary magazines as the *Kenyon Review, Sewanee Review, Virginia Quarterly Review, Shenandoah, Manoa, Ohio Review,* and *Prairie Schooner*, where she was awarded the Lawrence Foundation Prize for Fiction. In 2001, she received the Tate Prize for Poetry from the *Sewanee Review*. She was awarded one of the first Open Fellowships from the Lilly Endowment for a study of Inuit art and mythology and has held residencies at Yaddo, the Fundación Valparíso in Spain, Chateau de Lavigny in Switzerland, the Wurlitzer Foundation, and the Martha's Vineyard Writers' Residency. She has received various fellowships for residencies in painting at the Vermont Studio Center, where she has also been a Guest Writer.

SUSAN TEKULVE is the author of two story collections, *My Mother's War Stories* (Winnow Press) and *Savage Pilgrims* (Serving House Books). Her chapbook, *Wash Day*, appears in the "World Voices Series" at Webdelsol.com. Her stories, poems and essays have appeared in *Shenandoah, The Georgia Review, New Letters, Best New Writing 2007, The Indiana Review, Denver Quarterly, Puerto del Sol, Prairie Schooner, New Letters, Beloit Fiction Journal, Crab Orchard Review, The Literary Review, Web DelsSol, Black Warrior Review,* and *The Kansas City Star*. She has been awarded scholarships from the Bread Loaf

Writers' Conference and the Sewanee Writers' Conference. She teaches in the undergraduate and low-residency creative writing programs at Converse College.

SEAN TONER received his MFA from Fairleigh Dickinson in 2006. His writing has appeared at webdelsol.com, in *Opium Magazine* (where he's twice been a finalist in their 500-word memoir contest), and in a handful of winners anthologies from the Philadelphia Writers Conference. Sean later joined the board of the PWC and became its vice president. He has been sightless since 1995 and is a public speaker about disability. (Web: www.seantoner.com)

ELLEN VISSON arrived in Switzerland in 1983 with Philippe, a painter. They had no habitation permits and no money, obtained the former and fought constantly for the latter. Twenty-five years passed where they lived only from the sales of his paintings. Recently widowed, Ellen is a six-time Pushcart nominee and a finalist for the 2007 Eric Hoffer award. She has stories published or forthcoming in *Pleiades, The Literary Review, Ascent, The Chattahoochee Review, Hayden's Ferry Review, Tiferet, Hunger Mountain, Absinthe: New European Writing, descant, The Jabberwock Review, The MacGuffin, Best New Writing 2007, Existere, Quay, Rum Ellen inate, ByLine, The Journal of Irreproducible Results,* and *The American Drivel Review.*

WALLIS WILDE-MENOZZI has published a memoir, *Mother Tongue An American Life in Italy,* as well as numerous essays in journals like *Granta, Best Spiritual Essays,* and *Kenyon Review.* Her poetry appears regularly in *Notre Dame Review, Mississippi Review,* and *Malahat Review.* (Web: www: WallisWilde-Menozzi.com)

CPSIA information can be obtained at www.ICGtesting.com
Printed in the USA
LVOW07s2049270715

447816LV00002B/653/P